ANCIENT NUBIA

ANCIENT NUBIA

P. L. SHINNIE

KEGAN PAUL INTERNATIONAL
London and New York

First published in 1996 by
Kegan Paul International Limited
UK: P.O. Box 256, London WC1B 3SW, England
Tel: (0171) 580 5511 Fax: (0171) 436 0899
USA: 562 West 113th Street, New York, NY 10025, USA
Tel: (212) 666 1000 Fax: (212) 316 3100

Distributed by

John Wiley & Sons Ltd
Southern Cross Trading Estate
1 Oldlands Way, Bognor Regis,
West Sussex, PO22 9SA, England
Tel: (01243) 779 777 Fax: (01243) 820 250

Columbia University Press
562 West 113th Street
New York, NY 10025, USA
Tel: (212) 666 1000 Fax: (212) 316 3100

Phototypeset in Palatino
by Intype, London

Printed in Great Britain by TJ Press, Padstow, Cornwall

ISBN 0–7103–0517–6

British Library Cataloguing in Publication Data

Shinnie, P. L.
Ancient Nubia
I. Title
939.78

ISBN 0–7103–0517–6

US Library of Congress Cataloging in Publication Data
Shinnie, P. L.
Ancient Nubia / P. L. Shinnie.
150 pp. 23 cm.
Includes bibliographical references and index.
ISBN 0–7103–0517–6
1. Nubia—History. 2. Nubia—Antiquities. 3.Egypt—Antiquities.
4. Sudan—Antiquities. I. Title.
DT159.6.N83S55 1995
939'.78—dc20   95–15878
                                                          CIP

DEDICATED
TO MY WIFE
AMA OWUSUA

CONTENTS

———◆———

Preface   xv
Acknowledgements   xvii

1 THE GEOGRAPHY, ENVIRONMENT AND PEOPLE OF NUBIA   1

2 THE STONE AGES   17

3 THE A-GROUP AND FIRST CONTACTS WITH EGYPT   43

4 THE C-GROUP, KERMA AND THE BEGINNINGS OF URBAN LIFE   54

5 EGYPTIAN OCCUPATION IN THE NEW KINGDOM   78

6 THE GROWTH OF AN INDEPENDENT SUDANESE STATE; NAPATA   95
   AND MEROE

7 CHRISTIAN NUBIA AND THE COMING OF ISLAM   119

Bibliography   135
Index   141

PLATES

◆

Between pages 46 and 47

1a. View of Nile
1b. View of Nile with ruins on an island
2. Saquia wheel
3. Nubian woman
4a. Well in Bayuda desert
4b. Camel in Bayuda desert
5a. A-Group pots
5b. A-Group pots
6. A-Group pots
7a. A-Group burial
7b. A-Group clay figurines
8a. C-Group pots
8b. Kerma period knife
9. C-Group beads
10a. Kerma West Deffufa
10b. Kerma East Deffufa
11a. Kerma pots
11b. Kerma burial
12a. C-Group cemetery at Ashkeit
12b. Tumulus grave at Kerma
13. Statue of Senuwy
14a. The Semna cararact
14b. Uronarti
15. Pharaonic statue at Tombos

16a. Gubbat el Hawa, Aswan
16b. Elephantine island
17a. Fort at Sai island
17b. Temple of Tuthmosis III at Semna
18a. Soleb temple
18b. Gebel Barkal
19a. Abu Simbel temple
19b. Nubian prisoners, Abu Simbel
20a. Buhen fort
20b. Buhen fort
21a. Amara West town wall
21b. Amara West town street
22. Soleb temple
23. Barkal temple from top of the hill
24a. Pyramid of Taharqa at Nuri
24b. Nuri pyramids
25a. Air view of Meroe town
25b. The Lion temple at Naqa
26a. Meroe pyramids
26b. Air view of Meroe pyramids
27. Meroe excavations

28a. Axumite inscription
     from Meroe
28b. Tabo temple
29a. Old Dongola church
29b. Church of the Columns
     at Old Dongola
30. Christian period pots

31a. Mograka church
31b. Debeira West house
32a. Wooden figure of St
     Michael from Attiri
32b. Christian tombstone
     inscribed in Greek

Cover photograph Tomb of Huy

FIGURES

———◆———

1. Ground plans of modern Nubian houses 14
2. Decoration on Nubian house doorways 15
3. Chronological chart of prehistoric cultures 18
4. Acheulean hand axes 19
5. Old Stone Age implements 20
6. Mousterian tools 22
7. Middle Old Stone Age tools 23
8. Neolithic pot sherds 29
9. Artefacts from Shaheinab 34
10. Rock drawings at Abka 41
11. Gold-handled mace of the A-Group 49
12. Relief of King Djer near Wadi Halfa 52
13. Fortified C-Group village at Wadi el Sebua 57
14. C-Group grave 58
15. Plan of C-Group house 59
16. Plan of C-Group settlement at Amada 60
17. C-Group artefacts 61
18. Reconstruction of audience hall at Kerma 69
19. Reconstruction of sacrificial ram's head-dress 71
20. Plans of Egyptian fortresses of the Middle Kingdom 75
21. Kurgus boundary inscription 80
22. Plan of Buhen fortress 84
23. Plan of Sesebi town 88
24. Scene from tomb of Djehuty-hetep 90
25. Mound grave at Kurru 97
26. Gold nugget from Kurru 98
27. Section through Meroitic pyramid 108
28. Plan of religious buildings at Musawwarat es Sofra 110
29. Meroitic pots 115

30. Nubian writing   127
31. Nubian brick vault   131

MAPS

---◆---

1. Nubia in relation to the whole Nile valley   2
2. Nubia from first cataract to junction of Blue and White Niles   4
3. Neolithic sites   27
4. A-Group sites   45
5. Pan-Grave sites   66
6. Egyptian forts at the second cataract   74
7. The Napata area   96
8. Plan of Meroe town   107
9. The 'Island of Meroe'   109
10. Medieval Nubia   121

PREFACE

——————◆——————

This book is designed to provide a clear, up-to-date account of the past of Nubia (both in Egypt and the Sudan) from the earliest human activity known there in Old Stone Age times until the coming of Islam in the fourteenth–fifteenth centuries AD, based on over 45 years' experience of that country both as an archaeological civil servant and an academic. The archaeology and ancient history of Nubia has not been well known until very recently and the book is planned to fill a gap by making this story more widely known.

I have tried to show in non-technical language the main results of archaeological and historical research from the nineteenth-century beginning of such studies until the present day. For much of this time Nubia was an archaeological backwater, but excavations during the Aswan High Dam archaeological salvage campaign brought it to the world's attention and interest has grown, with several world-class museums opening exhibitions of their Nubian material.

The book aims to provide background and more detailed information on the Nubian past for the many whose interest has now been aroused. It describes the country and the people as well as giving details of the monuments and artefacts of the ancient Nubians and their fascinating culture which survived centuries of change and periods of foreign rule.

Calgary 1994

ACKNOWLEDGEMENTS

———◆———

All plates are taken from the author's collection except for the following which are reproduced by kind permission of the persons and institutions shown: 5a, 5b, 6, 7a, 7b, 8a, 8b and 9 courtesy of the Trustees of the British Museum; 11a, 11b and 28b Professor C. Bonnet; 13, 14a and 14b Museum of Fine Arts, Boston; 20a and 20b Egypt Exploration Society; 30 Professor W. Y. Adams; 32a Mr A. J. Mills.

All maps and figures are taken from the author's personal collection except where otherwise indicated in the text.

Note on transliteration: In Sudanese and Nubian names G is used for soft g as in 'ginger'; Q is used for hard g as in 'game'.

CHAPTER 1

THE GEOGRAPHY, ENVIRONMENT AND PEOPLE OF NUBIA

The land of Nubia stretching along the river Nile from the first cataract southwards has never been very closely or accurately defined. Strictly the name should only be used for that part of the Nile valley where the Nubian language is spoken today – that is from slightly north of the first cataract at Kom Ombo in Egypt to the small town of Debba lying between the third and fourth cataracts in the Sudan. Much of this area is now uninhabited as a result of the vast inundation forming Lake Nubia, its Sudan name, or Lake Nasser as it is called in Egypt, caused by the building of the various dams at Aswan, culminating in the High Dam completed in 1969, which finally drowned a beautiful and historic land which had formed part of Nubia for millennia. The name Nubia has been used in a much wider sense when dealing with the past and sometimes it has been used as almost coterminous with the 'Ancient Sudan', the area of the present Republic of the Sudan. This in no way implies that all the inhabitants were speakers of the Nubian language even though the term Nubian is frequently, if inaccurately, used for the inhabitants.

In this book Nubia is used to mean not only the part which is linguistically Nubian today but to include the Nile valley to the junction of the Blue and White Niles at Khartoum and for some 250 kilometres further up the Blue Nile to include both banks of the river as far as Sennar, the southern limit of Nubian civilization as far as is now known.

The origin of the term Nubia is not known for certain. The similarity of the word with Nuba occurs, as will be seen, in various ancient writings, and the Nobatae are known from the fifth and sixth centuries AD and later, suggesting a connection. Confusion is often caused by the use of the word Nuba (not Nubian) for the people of the hills which lie to the west of the Blue Nile at approximately 30° east and 11° 30′ north. The confusion is further

1

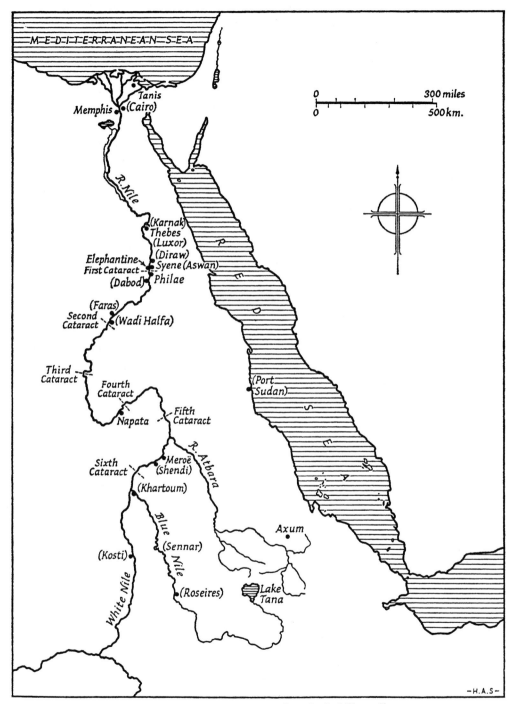

Map 1. Nubia in relation to the whole Nile valley

compounded since some of the several languages in this area are related to the Nubian spoken along the river in the more narrowly defined Nubia of today. It has been suggested that the name comes from the ancient Egyptian word *nbw*, meaning gold, since the area was an important source of gold in Pharaonic times and later, but it is not the name the ancient Egyptians used for the country and the suggestion may be fanciful. The Egyptians frequently called the area *Ta-sety*, 'Land of the Bow', or Kush, probably a name used by the inhabitants themselves. Nubians today tend to call themselves by terms which indicate the different dialects spoken – Kenuz, Mahas, Danagla – rather than to use Nubian as a general term, except when speaking in foreign languages, but the term Nobiin is increasingly being used to designate those who speak Mahas and other very closely related dialects.

The country itself is largely confined to the strip of cultivated land bounded by desert which borders the river, usually rainless in its northern part, but extending beyond the river banks once south of 17° 50' north, where annual rain can be expected and where signs of ancient human habitation are to be found at a considerable distance from the river. It must be understood that a description of the region reflects its appearance before the wholesale flooding after completion of the High Dam, since this can be described from living memory, but it should be noted that the original appearance of the country as known to those early inhabitants who are the subject of this book had already been changed by the building of the first dam in 1898–1902 and its subsequent heightenings in 1908–10 and 1929. The original landscape can only be restored for early prehistoric times by study of the geology and geomorphology, and for subsequent periods by the use of archaeological evidence and the descriptions and illustrations of early, mainly nineteenth-century, travellers.

The river, the dominant feature of the Nubian landscape, flows through a flat plain for over 2,000 kilometres from Sennar to Aswan, dropping less than 400 metres in the whole of that long journey. During the course of this journey, mostly through a valley cut through Nubian sandstone, the river flow is interrupted at six distinct places where igneous rocks of the basement complex have caused cataracts to form, from the first immediately up stream from Aswan to the sixth which is about 75 kilometres downstream from Khartoum. These cataracts have been a serious obstacle to river traffic and though boats can pass through them, with difficulty and danger, at the time of the annual Nile flood, as was done by the British and Egyptian troops during the military campaigns of 1885 and 1898, they have been a barrier to river traffic. Boats have tended only to be in general use within the various reaches of the river between the cataracts, and as a result many travellers, merchants and invaders journeyed mainly by land.

Following the course of the river Nile through the area defined here as

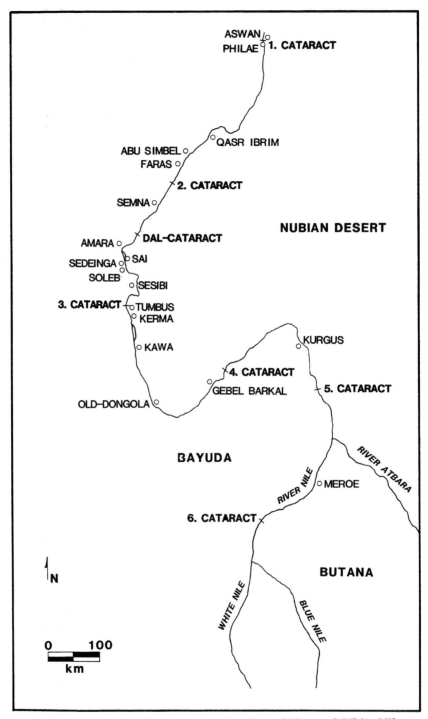

Map 2. Nubia from first cataract to junction of Blue and White Niles

Nubia, it starts on the Blue Nile at the modern town of Sennar (130° 34' north 33° 35' east) 250 kilometres up stream from its junction with the White Nile at Khartoum, from which place the single river flows over 2,000 kilometres through the Sudan and Egypt to reach the Mediterranean sea. Sennar has been chosen, as already mentioned, as the upstream boundary of Nubia since close to this town was found evidence of human occupation of Meroitic times and it is thus, until future exploration shows us more, the site of the furthest upstream dateable remains of the past. The White Nile is somewhat less known archaeologically but it is convenient to use latitude 12° 30' north to mark the southern limits of the area to be described.

The Blue and White Niles flow north past the clay plains of the Gezira (Arabic for island) which they enclose, making a rough triangle some 300 kilometres in height and with a base using the Kosti–Sennar railway line as a convenient datum, of 128 kilometres. This area and those on the east and west respectively of the two rivers consist of unconsolidated clay, silts, sand and gravels of varying depths. At its deepest it is 70 metres thick lying on Nubian sandstone. These deposits have been brought by the rivers and were probably laid down after the early Old Stone Age and certainly long before Neolithic times; radio carbon dates suggest that the deposits originated earlier than 10,000 BC.

The Blue Nile is joined by two tributaries flowing from the east, the Rahad and the Dinder, both these rivers deriving their water, as does the Blue Nile, from the summer rains of the Ethiopian plateau. In a year of plentiful rain the Dinder, especially, contributes much water to the annual flood, but in the dry season both rivers cease to flow and become a series of small ponds in a sandy bed.

The Blue Nile, arising in lake Tana in Ethiopia, is also dependent on the summer rains but its volume is far greater, and though its flow will vary from year to year there is always sufficient to provide some irrigation in the valley of the main Nile and, until the change in the flow pattern of the river caused by the building of dams from the late nineteenth century, it deposited fresh silt along the banks of the whole valley, thus making possible the agricultural development on which the civilization of ancient Egypt and much of Nubia was based.

The area enclosed by the two Niles, the Gezira already mentioned, receives rain, though in markedly varying quantities, every year and in previous centuries was important for grain production, mainly sorghum (Arabic *dura*), traditionally the main food crop of the central Sudan. Since the building of a dam at Sennar completed in 1925 and the introduction of perennial irrigation cotton has become the main crop and the economy of the modern country largely depends on it.

The White Nile, which rises in the lakes of central Africa, flows through similar flat country but has no tributaries in the area we are considering. It is much wider than the Blue Nile – up to 400 metres at Kosti and nearly 1 kilometre just before it reaches Khartoum, before the building of a dam at Gebel Auliya which has somewhat restricted it. This river carries less water than the Blue Nile, its flow is not so strong, and where the two rivers meet it is often ponded back by the stronger flow of the Blue Nile. The difference in colour of the waters of the two rivers – which gives rise to their names – can be clearly seen, the dark of the Blue Nile and the pale green of the White.

From this junction and the commencement of the main Nile a massive river runs through the country with evidence of old civilizations all along its banks. Except in the part known as the Butana, to be described later, human activity can only be traced in a narrow strip, seldom more than 2 kilometres wide, often much less. This activity was sometimes on both banks, but in some areas, where the desert has encroached and sand dunes have formed close to the river, only one bank has been exploited, though variation at different times in the past has changed the area of human occupation and agricultural activity from one bank to the other.

Eighty kilometres north of the river junction is the sixth cataract – the numbering of the cataracts is in the reverse direction to the flow of the river, the first cataract being at Aswan, the northern gate to Nubia. We shall in a more logical way describe the river in the direction in which it flows so that the sixth cataract is the first to be described. Frequently known as the Saba-loka, from a Nubian word for the drain pipes or waterspouts used to run water off the eaves of the houses, this cataract is formed of a mass of igneous rock, mainly granite and rhyolite, which has been cut through by the river to produce a dramatic gorge with rapids at the north end. The southern end of the gorge is overlooked by a hill, Gebel Rowyan, composed largely of granite and some 595 metres high, dominating the countryside.

Once past the Sabaloka the river takes a north-easterly direction and flows through the Shendi reach known from the name of the main town. This area, now the most densely inhabited part of the northern Sudan, has much rich alluvial soil making for productive agriculture on both banks of the Nile, though most settlement is on the east as it was in ancient times. The stretch of river goes as far as its junction with the river Atbara, the only tributary of the main Nile which flows from the south-east where it rises close to the Ethiopian border. It is highly seasonal and during the dry season is reduced to a series of pools.

Along this stretch of the Nile is found the one area with ancient buildings and ancient occupation at a distance from the river. It has already been said that rain falls in the area in most years, and in ancient times the vast region bounded by the Nile, the Blue Nile and the Atbara was the site of considerable activity, particularly in Meroitic times (c.750 BC–AD 350), and a number of monuments are to be found there. The region, a wide steppe-like territory with scattered acacia trees and plenty of grazing after the rains fall, has two distinct ecological zones with different names in present-day local use. Though frequently known as the 'Island of Meroe' by archaeologists following ancient usage, it is more accurate to define the two zones by using the current Arabic names. The western portion where the ancient Meroitic sites are found is primarily of Nubian sandstone and is known as the *Keraba*, whereas the *Butana*, a name often applied to the whole, refers specifically to the granite-based eastern portion where monumental remains have not been found, though traces of possible nomadic occupation are known.

Not far north of the junction of the Nile and the Atbara another region of cataract and rapids is reached where the basement complex lies in the line of the flow of the river. The fifth cataract itself is a little up stream of Bauga and roughly marks the point north of which rain very seldom falls and where, as a result, the cultivation of dates seriously begins. The whole stretch of river from here to Abu Hamed and beyond is a series of rapids with the river running in a narrow channel through hard rock, with many small islands and one large one, Mograt, at the point where the river changes its flow to the south-west. On none of these is the cultivable land able to support more than a very small population though throughout there are plenty of traces of earlier occupation, mainly of medieval and later times.

The small town of Abu Hamed is at the point where the Nile turns sharply to flow south-west for some 200 kilometres. Formerly it was important as the southern end of a much used camel caravan route which came across the desert from Kalabsha in Lower Nubia, cutting off the bend of the Nile and reducing the journey to less than 500 kilometres, a considerable saving as compared with the distance by the river route. With the development of the railway as part of the Anglo-Egyptian invasion of the Sudan in 1898 a modified form of this route was developed, from Wadi Halfa to Abu Hamed and on to Khartoum. Abu Hamed, although it remained a railway junction, lost its importance as a major staging post.

From Abu Hamed downstream is a stretch of about 200 kilometres of extremely rough and desolate country where many small islands and rapids and rock formations of biotite-gneiss make river navigation virtually impossible. The cultivable land is much restricted and the population small. This area is the least known stretch of the river in the whole of Nubia and only the most preliminary archaeological survey has been carried out. Proposals for a dam at the downstream end of this stretch of river have led to discussion to plan for the organization of a full archaeological salvage project. Below the cataract the river emerges from the zone of igneous rocks to flow once more through sandstone where an occasional uneroded isolated hill is seen, of which the largest is Gebel Barkal, on the right bank close to the modern town of Karima. This highly noticeable hill was taken to be of sacred importance in pharaonic times and later, and it became a cult centre with many temples in the vicinity.

Several normally dry watercourses (Arabic *wadi*) join the Nile in this area. After heavy summer rains these will flow for a short time with water and the Wadi Abu Dom which drains from the Bayuda desert, the area within the bend of the river, has on occasion brought destructive floods to Merowe (not to be confused with the ancient town of Meroe), the small town which lies at its mouth.

Seventy-five kilometres down stream of the fourth cataract, near the town of Korti, the river turns once more to resume its northward flow, thus completing a great double bend. Flowing in the quiet stretch of the Dongola reach, named from the main town of the region, for about 400 kilometres through a region of sandstone where the right bank is heavily encroached on by sand dunes, the river traverses well cultivated alluvial plains with considerable population close to the river banks, whilst away from the river are treeless desert plains of sand and gravel. This Dongola reach flows to the third cataract where the river turns east for a short distance to traverse the biotite-gneiss rocks of the cataract. From here on date palms become common and are especially plentiful close to the cataract – this district is today the main date-producing region of the Sudan.

After the river turns north again there are large areas of alluvium on the right bank where the towns of Abri and Delgo are to be found, whilst on the opposite bank are traces of ancient occupation now largely covered with sand dunes. This stretch of river is largely unimpeded until after 200 kilometres the Dal cataract is reached, marking the southern limit of a stretch of 160 kilometres of rough water dotted with islands and igneous rock formations with one exceptionally narrow gap at Semna. This gap is about 50 metres wide and at low water the whole flow of the river passes through it. This area, known as the *Batn el Hagar* in Arabic or *Kidin Tu* in Nubian, means the 'Belly of the Rocks' and is an appropriate term for a region of extreme desolation with only a few small villages and tiny agricultural plots, usually irrigated by lifting water from the river by means of the ox-driven water wheel known in Arabic as *saqia* and in Nubian as *eskalay* (Plate 2). Since this device was not introduced until the last few centuries BC the earlier agricultural potential of the area must have been very limited unless there has been a considerable alteration in the river level. There is evidence for some changes in level but it does not seem that they were sufficiently great to have made a marked difference in the capacity of the area to support a large population. After 160 kilometres the second cataract proper is reached and here, close to modern Wadi Halfa, the most northerly town of the Sudan, is another major obstacle where again granite outcrops bar the free flow of the river for about 20 kilometres.

North of the second cataract and as far as the first cataract at Aswan, with the exception of the stretch from Kalabsha to Aswan, 56 kilometres long, through which there are rocky outcrops, the river runs through a level flood plain with many areas of good soil and a considerable agricultural potential with many traces of ancient occupation. The broad and easily navigated stretch of river was a major waterway and continued to be so used until the building of the High Dam. This area lies within the boundaries of Egypt, and Egyptian or Lower Nubia bears many resemblances to Upper Egypt north of Aswan. It presented no serious obstacle to Egyptian penetration in ancient times and Egyptians settled there would not have felt it as alien as the region beyond the second cataract. Occupied by the Egyptians at various times in the past, Lower Nubia became in a formal sense part of modern Egypt when the present frontier was established at the end of the nineteenth century. In both ancient and modern times any definition of the culture, in the broadest sense, of this area would include it with the rest of Nubia which now lies in the Sudan. The first cataract was certainly regarded by the ancient Egyptians as their southern frontier and Abu, the town on the island known as Elephantine (*Abu* means elephant in Egyptian) was the southernmost town of Egypt to be joined in late pharaonic times by Aswan (from Egyptian *swnw*, meaning 'trade' or 'market'), the town which stands on the east bank opposite the island and which came to be of greater importance than the town on the island, at least from Ptolemaic times.

RESOURCES

As a description of the geography of the Nile indicates, the natural resources of the area are not great and the population has maintained itself almost entirely with agriculture and the production of food stuffs, mostly grown for local consumption. The river has supplied the water for crop growing throughout Nubia except in the rain-fed *wadis* of the Keraba and the clay plain of the Gezira. As already suggested, in many of the more northern areas cultivable soil would have been severely restricted before the introduction of the water wheel.

The cereal crop which has provided the mainstay of the diet certainly for centuries, almost certainly for millennia, is sorghum, used to make a flat, unleavened, pancake-life loaf (Arabic *kisra*) eaten with a sauce of vegetables and on occasion meat. Sorghum is also used to make a porridge-like dish (Arabic *asida*). It is a crop which grows well with summer rain and the southern parts of Nubia are ideal for its production though it will also grow on what is known as 'seluka' land – so called from the Nubian name, also used in Sudan Arabic, for the wooden digging stick with which holes are made in the freshly deposited silt along the lower parts of the river banks into which are sown the seeds of sorghum. Where conditions require it is also grown on land irrigated by the water wheel, known as 'saqia' land. Direct evidence of the use of sorghum is to be found in its presence in archaeological contexts in a number of places from Meroitic times stretching from Qasr Ibrim in the north to Meroe in the south, and a depiction of a head of sorghum is to be seen in the hand of the Meroitic ruler carved in the rock at Gebel Qeili in the Butana south-east of Khartoum. In addition to sorghum it can be assumed that millet (*pennisetum*) (Arabic *dukhn*) was grown as it is today on the poorer soils, though it is much less popular as human food than sorghum.

In the most northern parts of Nubia wheat, which requires winter watering, is grown and today largely takes the place of sorghum as a main dietary item, being used in much the same way as sorghum to make flat cakes known in Nubian as *wirikeen*. Wheat and barley have both been found at Qasr Ibrim where the conditions make the chance of survival exceptionally favourable. It can be assumed that, as in Egypt, wheat was used for bread and barley for beer, though barley is not so used today and very little is grown, much of it being used as fodder for horses and donkeys. One example of fox-tailed millet, *Sitaria italica*, has been found in a medieval context at Hambukol near to Dongola.

In addition to the main cereal crops a small range of other plant food was grown. Beans of several kinds are known – cow pea (*Vigna unguiculata*, Arabic *lubia helu*) is the most common. Of green vegetables the indigenous ones which will have been available in ancient times are okra (*Hibiscus esculentus*, Arabic *bamia*), much used as a sauce to eat with *kisra*, as well as cress (*Eruca sativa*, Arabic *girgir*), purslane (*Portulaca oleracea*, Arabic *rigla*), lettuce (widely used in ancient Egypt and regarded as an aphrodisiac), onions and garlic. The most common vegetable now, and probably in ancient times, is Jew's mallow (*Corchorus olitorius*, Arabic *mulukhiya*). The tomato, now widely used in the Sudanese diet, is a New World crop and was only introduced rather recently.

Dates are and were widely grown and formed an important part of the diet – in dried form they are well adapted for use on desert journeys. There seems not to have been other cultivated fruits until various kinds of citrus were introduced in recent times, but a number of wild fruits are now eaten and surely were in the past, notably those known as *lalob*, the fruit of the *heglig* tree (*Balanites aegyptiaca*) and *nebaq* from the *sidr* (*Zizyphus spinachristi*). Alcoholic drinks were made of sorghum for the widespread African beer, *merisa* in the Sudan, and dates also provided the juice from which other alcoholic drinks were made.

Meat, both beef, mutton and goat, was available but was, as nowadays, used sparingly and only on special occasions. At Meroe, where the Keraba grazing area was available for large herds of cattle, beef in particular was plentiful. Milk was drunk and played a part in ceremonial life. In northern Nubia pigs were kept in Christian times. They seem not to have been kept by the Meroites and they disappear with the coming of Islam.

Camels and donkeys were the beasts of burden as today, but the camel is a comparatively recent addition to the domestic fauna – it is not represented until Meroitic times and then infrequently, but it has recently been shown that there is evidence for a rather earlier introduction of the animal at Qasr Ibrim where a mandible and dung pellets have been found in a context which suggests a date in the early Napatan period. Horses were known and are depicted. They were in use for ceremonial purposes and were probably reserved for the élite, and to pull chariots rather than to be ridden.

Of non-edible crops cotton now is important and for many years has been the mainstay of the Sudan's economy. It is mainly grown in the Gezira but there is some cultivation further north. Cotton was known and used for textiles in ancient Nubia but perhaps not earlier than Meroitic times. At Qasr Ibrim the earliest evidence is from Roman times. It is not known where it was grown but probably in many small-scale schemes. By the eighteenth century AD the making of cotton cloth had been sufficiently developed for it to be used as currency.

This brief description of geography and geomorphology is of the country as it was prior to the building of the dams starting with the first Aswan dam of 1898. Although changes in water level of the river will have made slight changes and there may have been periods in which the northern limit of the summer rain has been farther north than it is now, the appearance of the country has been very much the same throughout Holocene times. It has been convincingly suggested that vegetation belts, a good indicator of the quantity of rainfall, were 250 kilometres north of their present position just before the well known decrease of rainfall in about 3000 BC. In pre-Holocene times the situation will have been different and some indication of the nature and régime of the river is given in the chapter dealing with the Stone Age.

Current climate gives an impression of that of earlier times. Much of the area, that to the north of latitude 19° north, has a typical desert climate with extremely hot, dry summers with a mean maximum temperature of 41.3°C at Wadi Halfa in June (though 52.5°C was recorded in the same month in 1903) and a mean minimum of 23.1°C. The winters, lasting approximately from November to February, have a cool dry climate with mean maximum of 24°C at Wadi Halfa in January and a minimum of 7.8°C. The winters vary considerably depending on the amount and strength of wind from the north and 0°C has been recorded at Wadi Halfa. Further south the rains of summer and the hot and humid season after the rain shows different temperatures and Khartoum has a mean maximum in June of 41.1°C, a minimum of 26.1°C. In January Khartoum has a mean maximum of 32.1°C and a minimum of 15.2°C. The relative humidity ranges from 51% at Wadi Halfa in January to 22% in June and in Khartoum from 36% to 38% for the same months.

THE PEOPLE

The term Nubian today refers only to those who speak the Nubian language and that, as already mentioned, is restricted to only part of the area whose past history and antiquities are being described. In spite of difference of language the physical appearance and the modern Islamic culture of the people is very similar throughout the whole region and it is only over the last five hundred years or so that the language of the southern part of Nubia has changed. In the northern part of Nubia the Nubian language is spoken, a member of an important family of African languages known as Eastern Sudanic, stretching from the Nubian-speaking part of the Nile valley as far as the language of the Masai of East Africa and including the Nilotic languages spoken by Shilluk, Dinka and Nuer peoples of the southern Sudan as well as others. The Eastern Sudanic language group forms a part of the wider grouping known as Nilo-Saharan. Related Nubian languages may have had a wide currency in north-east Africa in ancient times and remnants of them are now to be seen in the Nubian spoken along the river as well as in some languages of the Nuba hills in south-east Kordofan, and Meidobi, Birgid and Daju spoken far to the west of the Nile. Most scholars of the subject consider that the origin of the Nubian language lay in the area of Darfur and Kordofan and that it spread from there to the river. If this is so then there would have been a continuous belt of related languages across the Sudan which has been divided and broken up by the introduction of other languages, mainly Arabic, since the end of medieval times. It is suggested that the split between the different Nubian languages took place more than 2,500 years ago but there is no knowledge of when the ancestor of the present-day river Nubian language arrived in the Nile valley nor of whether it was present there in Meroitic and earlier times or whether it arrived in the early centuries AD to supplant Meroitic.

River Nubian, whose ancestor Old Nubian is known in written form from many documents of medieval date, is now spoken in three clearly differentiated dialects along the Nile. From north to south these are Kenuz, formerly spoken from Aswan to Aniba but whose speakers have almost all been transplanted, mostly to Kom Ombo north of Aswan, as a result of the flooding of their homeland by the High Dam. Further south are the speakers of several very closely related dialects conveniently known as Fadija-Mahas, Fadija referring to those who lived in the northern part who, like the Kenuz, are now mostly moved, whereas the Mahas are to be found in territory up stream of the flood to past the third cataract nearly to Kerma, where traditionally the shrine known as Abu Fatma marks the boundary between Mahas and the third group, Dongolawi, which terminates at Debba. A curious feature of the dialect distribution is that Kenuz and Dongolawi, which are so close as to be virtually the same dialect, are to north and south, with Fadija-Mahas in the middle. No satisfactory explanation has so far been adduced for this unusual distribution.

Arabic, now the official language of the Sudan, has had a major impact since about the fifteenth century AD. Up stream of Debba it has replaced Nubian, and Arabic is now spoken not only in the river valley but throughout the central Sudan. Nubian was in use, at least by the riverain population, as far as the junction of the Blue and White Niles until about 500 years ago, as is shown by the presence of inscriptions in Old Nubian and by the existence of Nubian place names, as well as the survival of a number of Nubian words in the colloquial Arabic of the present agricultural population. It cannot be said with certainty for how long Nubian has been spoken in the Nile valley. It may have a long history even going back to Neolithic times, or it may be a comparatively recent introduction following on the collapse of the Meroitic state in the mid-fourth century AD, or it may have arrived at any time in between. Present information does not make it possible to have any certainty nor to understand by what process the language was introduced to the Nile valley.

The Nubian people, on evidence from the study of ancient skeletal remains, seem to have been of a very stable physical type and little change is to be seen over thousands of years. The appearance of modern Nubians, including the Arabic speakers in the southern part, gives a reasonable indication of the physical attributes of their ancestors. The Nile valley population shows a gradual change from the rather light-skinned people of northern Egypt to the very dark ones of the southern Sudan and various combinations of these physical features are to be seen throughout Nubia. The majority of the riverside population are brown-skinned, of medium height and with hair varied from straight to curly. They tend to prognathism and to aquiline features but the long period of contact with negro peoples to the south results in many individuals with negroid appearance. There are sufficient representations of Nubians from ancient times to support the skeletal evidence and to show ancient Nubians as an African people fundamentally the same as modern ones (Plate 3).

The coming of Arabs from as early as the ninth century, and in increasing numbers from the fourteenth century, has had a powerful linguistic, religious and cultural impact but has, in spite of a new genetic element, not had a great influence on the appearance of the people, though it must have increased the variability of physical appearance.

One cultural trait which has persisted since at least Meroitic times and which implies that the same people have continued to live in Nubia is that of facial scarification. Now dying out, various patterns of face scars can still be seen amongst the riverain population. Different patterns are identified with different modern groups such as the three parallel horizontal scars on each cheek for the Shaigiya, a people of the region down stream of the fourth cataract, and three vertical scars amongst the Jaaliyyin who inhabit the stretch of river running past Meroe from Khartoum to Atbara. Many Meroitic representations of these facial scars are known.

The general way of life, until very recently, has been the same during much of Nubian history. Crops and diet, as already described, have persisted unchanged, and although wheat bread has become a preferred basic food of town dwellers, country people still eat sorghum *kisra* and *asida*. An agricultural population growing all the ancient crops to which some new ones (maize, tomatoes, ground nuts and tobacco being amongst the most important) have been added has not changed its way of life in any substantial way. Still close to the soil, the Nubian works hard on his small plots of land and until the recent introduction of cash crops such as cotton the cultivation was mainly a subsistence one.

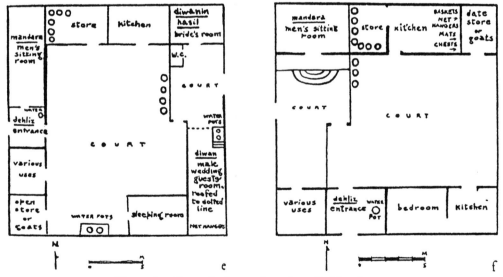

Figure 1. Ground plans of modern Nubian houses
(*from* M. Wenzel, *House Decoration in Nubia*, London, 1972)

14

Figure 2. Decoration on Nubian house doorways
(*from* M. Wenzel, *House Decoration in Nubia*, London, 1972)

Houses, mainly of sun-dried mud brick or of *terre pisée* (Arabic *galus*), are now larger than in ancient times, especially in Nubia proper where large courtyard houses have been the fashion for the last seventy years or so. These flat-roofed houses are to be seen throughout Nubia, those in the north being more spacious than those of the central Sudan. In the extreme north, amongst the Kenuz, the flat-roofed houses do not occur and the local people still build, in mud brick, smaller, narrow-roomed houses with barrel-vaulted roofs exactly as was done in medieval times throughout Nubia.

Some dwellings are still to be seen of earlier types and some of the nomadic and transhumant peoples live in matting-covered huts whose prototype may go back to Neolithic times. Similar structures are also erected by dwellers in more substantial houses to serve as animal shelters and for shelter against the sun on informal occasions.

CHAPTER 2

THE STONE AGES

———————◆———————

The first dated evidence for humans in Nubia during the Old Stone Age is possibly 300,000 years ago. By 70,000 BC the forerunners of modern man, *Homo sapiens*, would have been present. They are known only from the stone tools that have survived from that period, the most characteristic of which are known as Acheulean 'hand axes' (named from the town of Acheul in France where such tools were first found). These are large unspecialized tools, of roughly pear shape, whose exact use is not known, though we assume them to have had a range of function much of which would be concerned with the dismemberment and skinning of animals caught in the chase for food. These hand axes first appeared in Africa, the earliest in the world, about perhaps 1.5 million years ago, but reached the Nile valley much later. No doubt these early people also used wooden objects such as spears and clubs but no traces of them are known from Nubia and our knowledge of the first inhabitants of the Nubian Nile valley is derived solely from a study of the stone implements.

The earliest examples of tools so far known for this period are the 'hand axes' of the Khor Abu Anga type, named from a site close to Khartoum, and similar tools have been found throughout Nubia where the best studied area is around Wadi Halfa. In addition to 'hand axes' other simple tools, also made by removing flakes from a stone core, known as 'ovates' and 'choppers', are found. These scanty remains of human activity have been mainly found in what are assumed to be the workshops where the tools were made, or in quarries where ferricrete sandstone, the material from which the tools were made, was obtained. Few dwelling sites have been found and there is little to inform us of the way of life of the makers of the tools. They must certainly have hunted, though we do not have bones from the animals they hunted to enable us to be sure what animals they were eating. Evidence from other

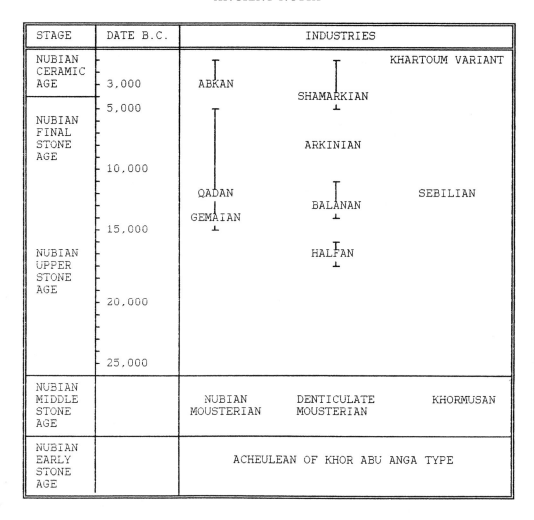

STAGE	DATE B.C.	INDUSTRIES		
NUBIAN CERAMIC AGE	3,000	ABKAN	SHAMARKIAN	KHARTOUM VARIANT
NUBIAN FINAL STONE AGE	5,000 10,000	QADAN GEMAIAN	ARKINIAN BALANAN	SEBILIAN
NUBIAN UPPER STONE AGE	15,000 20,000 25,000		HALFAN	
NUBIAN MIDDLE STONE AGE		NUBIAN MOUSTERIAN	DENTICULATE MOUSTERIAN	KHORMUSAN
NUBIAN EARLY STONE AGE		ACHEULEAN OF KHOR ABU ANGA TYPE		

Figure 3. Chronological chart of prehistoric cultures

parts of the world suggests that they were capable of successfully hunting large mammals. They also foraged for vegetable foods and the 'hand axes' may have been used for digging out roots as well as for butchering animals. At this time the Nile had already been established in approximately its modern form and its presence was an important factor in determining human adaptation to the environment.

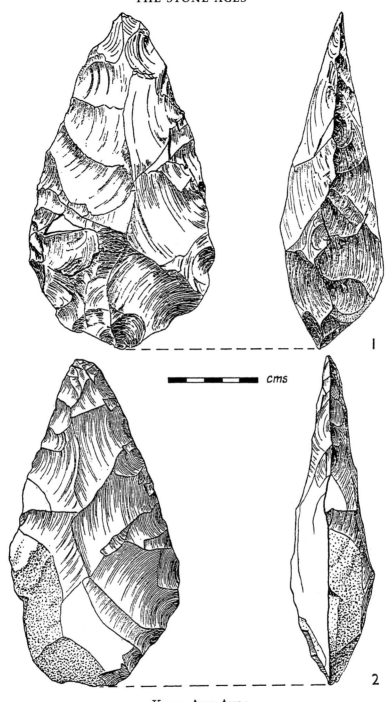

cms

1

2

KHOR ABU ANGA
Figure 4.   Acheulean hand axes
(*from* A. J. Arkell, *The Old Stone Age in the Anglo-Egyptian Sudan*, Khartoum, 1949)

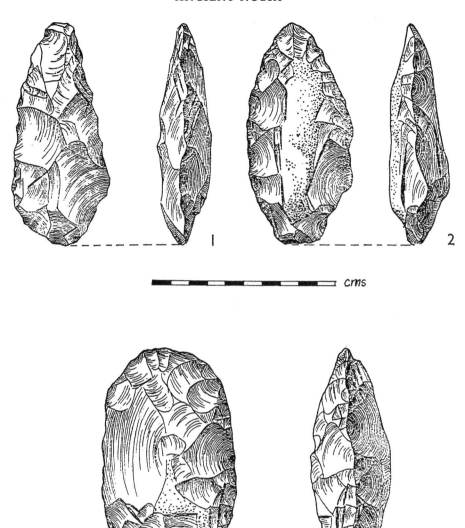

KHOR ABU ANGA

Figure 5. Old Stone Age implements
(*from* A. J. Arkell, *The Old Stone Age in the Anglo-Egyptian Sudan*, Khartoum, 1949)

During the succeeding Middle Stone Age, which is dated to more than 40,000 years ago, there is a greater variety of stone tools, and though 'hand axes' continued to be made and used, a greater skill was achieved in the removal of flakes from blocks of stone to produce the required result. We do not know if the makers of the tools were descendants of those who made the

Acheulean 'hand axes' or if they were newcomers bringing new techniques with them. No gradual transition from Acheulean to the Middle Stone Age can be seen, which suggests a new stone-working tradition and perhaps supports the view that a new group of people entered Nubia at the time, though it cannot be said from where they may have come.

The following description of the Middle Stone Age cultures of Nubia is largely based on the analysis given by Wendorf in his conclusion to the two volumes of detailed results of field work by the Combined Prehistoric Expedition to Nubia which worked in the 1960s as part of the UNESCO sponsored campaign to 'Save the Monuments of Nubia'. Changes have been suggested to some aspects of these results, particularly by Yousif el Amin and Fekri Hassan.

Three distinct 'industries', or different styles of stone working, have been defined for Nubia: First is the 'Nubian Mousterian' which is dated by its resemblance to material from Europe and the Near East to about 45,000 to 33,000 BC. 'Hand axes' were still made but a variety of other smaller tools were also in use, scrapers, points and burins, which are small chisel shaped tools probably used for working bone. The ability to make these smaller tools depended on working flakes which had been detached from a large piece of stone and was due to the development of what is known as the Levallois technique, by which the original stone nucleus was carefully trimmed by the removal of flakes in a planned way to produce flakes which could themselves be used as tools – often as blades, since such flakes had very sharp edges, but also cores of a pre-determined shape which could be used in a variety of ways. All tools continued to be made of ferricrete sandstone, no other material being easily available. The first small settlement sites to have been found date from this period, and quarry and workshop sites are also known.

The second industry is known as the 'Denticulate Mousterian' from the presence of flake tools with denticulations, that is notches rather like saw teeth, along the edges. These saw-like tools may have been used for wood working. Only two sites, both small, compact settlements, are known for this industry and they may well be of the same date and of the same people as the 'Nubian Mousterian' but representing some specialized activity.

The third industry is the 'Nubian Middle Palaeolithic' and it shows quite different characteristics both in type of tools and in the technology for making them. The industry resembles the Sangoan/Lupemban of central and east Africa, though it does not have the 'pick'-like tools which are characteristic of the Sangoan. Otherwise it has a range of small tools. These three industries cannot be separated chronologically at present. They may well have been contemporary or may have succeeded each other in the period of about 50,000 years which they span.

In addition to these three distinct industries it seems that the Khormusan,

21

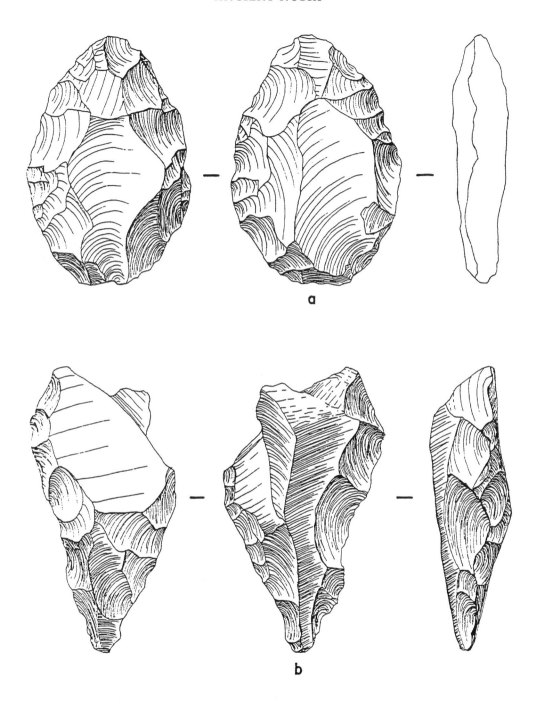

Figure 6.   Mousterian tools
(from F. Wendorf, *The Prehistory of Nubia,* Fort Burgwin, 1968)

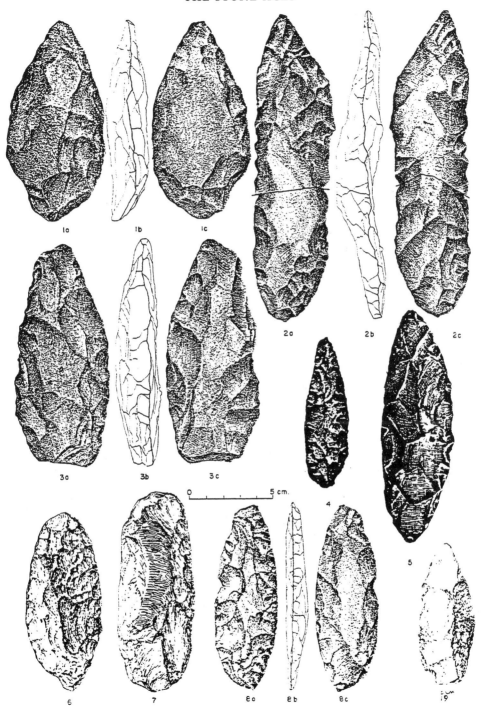

Figure 7. Middle Old Stone Age tools
(*from* F. Wendorf, *The Prehistory of Nubia*, Fort Burgwin, 1968)

originally thought to belong to the Upper Stone Age, should be included here. At one time dated to c.25,000–16,000 BC it is now known to be more than 40,000 years old and should be placed in the Middle Paleolithic.

Three main classes of artefacts largely made by the Levallois technique are flakes, burins and denticulates, and these tools are marked by a change from the predominant use of sandstone, as in earlier times, to that of chert, a stone which is more tractable and can be more easily flaked. It seems that these people were hunting large animals and were also fishing. It is now suggested that the Khormusan and the 'Nubian Mousterian' perhaps ended by c.40,000 BC. If contemporary it may be that Mousterian and Khormusan assemblages represent two different cultural groups, but Yousif el Amin suggests that variation in tool styles more probably reflects a difference of 'adaptive strategies of interrelated communities rather than true cultural differences'. Since there is a lack of data for the environment or for the activities of the makers of these tools any attempt to reconstruct their life is almost impossible.

Some of the Khormusan sites have very large numbers of burins, in some cases half of the total number of tools. As already mentioned, it has usually been considered that burins, with their chisel-shaped ends, were used for working bone, but in these sites there is very little evidence for use on bone. It may be that they were also used for working wood, and since these sites were along the river bank where wood would have been plentiful the burins could have been so used – the wood itself has not survived to give a certain answer.

The 'Nubian Upper Stone Age' follows, and by some time after about 20,000 BC the Nile valley, which had assumed its present bed long before, had developed an environment closely similar to that of the present day.

During this period several different industries have been identified, mainly in the Wadi Halfa area, covering the period from about 20,000 to 9000 BC. They have been named from places where type sites were found, and are distinguished from each other by variations in the styles of stone implements and of the techniques by which they were made. So far only the Wadi Halfa region has been examined in detail and the identification of industries and the general conclusions drawn from their study may not be applicable in other parts of Nubia.

The Khormusan was followed from c.15,500–13,000 BC by the Gemaian, seen in a number of small camps, perhaps for hunting, along the channels of the Nile. The tools, burins (which are rare), pointed flakes, scrapers and denticulates, were of chert, and these people also were hunters of large savanna-type animals. In the contemporary Halfan the stone industry was dominated by microlithic blades.

The Sebilian, known from Upper Egypt as well as Nubia, shows considerable differences. These tools are once again made from sandstone and are larger and less finely made. For some time it was thought, because of the nature of stone technology, that the Sebilian was contemporary with the Middle Stone Age and dated to c.13,000–9000 BC. To explain this appearance of an anachronistic industry it has been suggested that there was an immigration of people with a different culture from the south, and analogies can be seen between material of the Sebilian and of the Tshitolian of central Africa. However new research throws considerable doubt on the validity of these dates and the Sebilian may be much earlier. If this is so some of the problems of the supposedly archaic technology would be removed.

NUBIAN FINAL OLD STONE AGE

In the final stages of the Old Stone Age very small stone tools known as microliths predominate. These small tools were mainly components of tools and weapons of other materials such as wood and bone, and the microliths were used as arrow heads, as knife blades, as scrapers probably mounted in wooden handles, and as tools for cutting plants – the forerunners of the sickles with which cereal crops would be harvested in the future. Five different industries have been defined in Lower Nubia distinguished by varying types of tools. The oldest is that known as the Halfan, dated to approximately 18,000–15,000 BC and thus overlapping in date the Gemaian and possibly co-existing with it for a while. Small camp sites have been found and the main means of subsistence was still by hunting and fishing. By the time of the Qadan the grinding of wild cereal grains had been developed, shown by the large number of grinding stones found. The presence of silica sheen on lunates indicates that they were being used as sickles in the collecting of wild grains. The Halfan is followed by the Ballanan (c.14,000–12,000 BC) and the Qadan (c.12,500–9000 BC) in which for the first time cemeteries have been found. The burials were in shallow, oval pits, some of them within the camp sites, and all were buried in a flexed attitude with hands close to the face. One cemetery, at Gebel Sahaba, contained skeletons showing evidence of injuries caused by stone weapons. They are the first examples of war dead from Nubia.

Then, in probable chronological order, came the Arkinian, known only from one site dated to 7440 ± 180 BC and the Shamarkian with dates ranging from 5750 to 3270 BC. All these industries are characterized by microlithic tools of varying types and are distinguished from one another by stylistic variations. These last two industries have a close resemblance to the well known Capsian of North Africa and there may have been contact between the people of the Nile valley and those of north Africa through the Sahara. It should be observed that very little information is available for the Palaeolithic period in parts of Nubia other than the area studied by the American-led Combined Prehistoric Expedition which is that now flooded by the Aswan High Dam. Arkell, who discovered the Acheulean site at Khor Abu Anga already referred to, found stone tools in a number of places in Nubia, but these were chance finds and no occupation sites were found. Following the Combined Prehistoric Expedition's work in the flood salvage area a survey was made in the region of Debba (still unpublished) with meagre results, and a subsequent survey in the Shendi region found no palaeolithic sites. It seems on present evidence that whilst at least Late Palaeolithic people were living in considerable numbers north of the second cataract they did not occupy land to the south.

THE NEW STONE AGE OR NEOLITHIC PERIOD

The people of the Old Stone Age got their livelihood exclusively from hunting, fishing and collecting of food stuffs but as time went on improved techniques of control over the environment were made possible by the variety and increased specialization of stone tools and by the development of microliths which were used in composite tools such as arrows. The finding of arrow heads is good evidence for the use of the bow and the development of this weapon made possible more successful hunting strategies than had been possible before.

Other techniques of producing a food supply began to develop, probably starting with the domestication of cattle, sheep and goats so that a permanent supply of milk, meat and other animal products such as bone and leather were always available and the need for hunting was much reduced. Similarly it was discovered that some of the wild vegetable resources, particularly of wild grasses, could be obtained by saving the seeds and planting them near the encampments. Once this became a common practice the need for continual movement in search of food supplies was made unnecessary and more permanent settlements became established. Together with these new ways of providing sustenance went the discovery that it was possible to make containers of various shapes and sizes from clay and to make pottery by subjecting the clay to heat. This discovery, probably by much trial and error, not only supplied humankind with containers which were superior to the previous ones of basket and gourd but also left a large supply of virtually indestructible material for archaeologists to find. This material, pottery, was shaped and decorated in many different ways at different times in the past and responded to changes in fashion in a way which could be analysed by archaeologists and used to define different groups of people and sometimes to arrange them in chronological order.

26

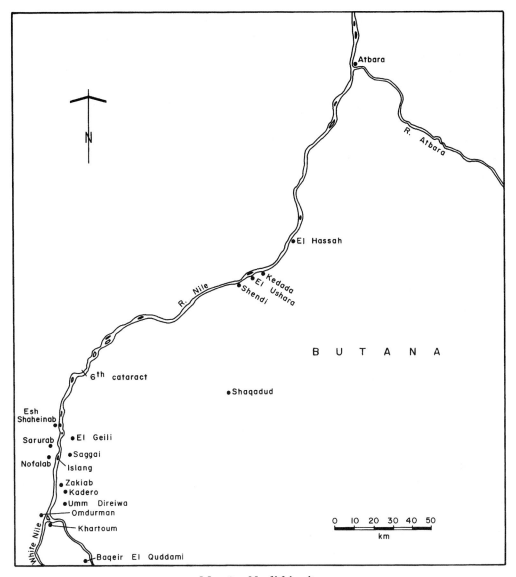

Map 3. Neolithic sites

In Nubia the best studied area for this new development is close to the junction of the Blue and White Niles. In this area many Neolithic sites have been found since A.J. Arkell first worked there in 1944, and both banks of the Nile north from Khartoum have been surveyed and sites excavated during recent years. To the south of Khartoum less is known but a few sites have now been investigated.

Arkell discovered the first known site of the central Sudan neolithic when he excavated at the site of the Khartoum hospital. Here he found the earliest pottery-making culture so far known and defined it by the characteristic 'wavy line' patterns on the pottery so that at first he named it the 'Wavy Line culture' and later called it the 'Khartoum Mesolithic', a name still found in many publications, though it is somewhat misleading since Mesolithic has a very precise meaning for European prehistory but is not usually used in Africa. Perhaps to call it the 'Early Khartoum' culture is best since the name gives the place of discovery without committing the material to any other preconceived cultural entity.

When originally found there was no means of obtaining any precise date, though it was obvious from the material found that it was likely to be earlier than the beginning of early dynastic times in Egypt, the only place from which a chronology could be obtained. It would, therefore, be earlier than c.3,000 BC. Now, with carbon-14 dates available from other sites of the same period, the date is seen to range between c.6500 BC and 5000 BC, though dates from a site at Sarurab on the west bank of the Nile suggest that 'Early Khartoum' people may have been there as early as the eighth millennium BC.

Since the discovery and excavation of the Khartoum hospital site several others have been identified and examined, at Tagra and Shabona on the White Nile south of Khartoum, at Saggai and Sarurab on the east and west banks respectively of the main Nile, and in the one non-riverain site so far known, at Shaqadud.

These sites show a distinctive pottery with wavy line decoration as well as other impressed decoration, one of which was described by the excavator as 'dotted wavy line'. The wavy line, so characteristic of the pottery of the time, was made by using the barbed spine of the catfish (*Synadontis schall*) as a comb on the wet clay. In addition to the ceramics there was a well developed microlithic stone industry, most of the tools being made from quartz with many lunates; small crescent-shaped flakes almost certainly used as arrow heads, scrapers and other pieces. There were also harpoons made of bone and small pierced stones thought to be net sinkers.

The settlements of these people as so far known are all, with the exception of Shaqadud, located on the river bank, though no traces of their dwellings have been found. The animal bones provide evidence for the presence of animals which would have been more at home in a climate that was considerably wetter than it is now and show that hunting and fishing formed an important part of the subsistence. Amongst these animals a reed rat had originally been assumed to belong to a new species and was named *Thryonomys arkelli* (Arkell's reed rat) after the excavator. It is now considered not to be a new or separate species but to be the standard Marsh Cane Rat (*Thryonomys*

28

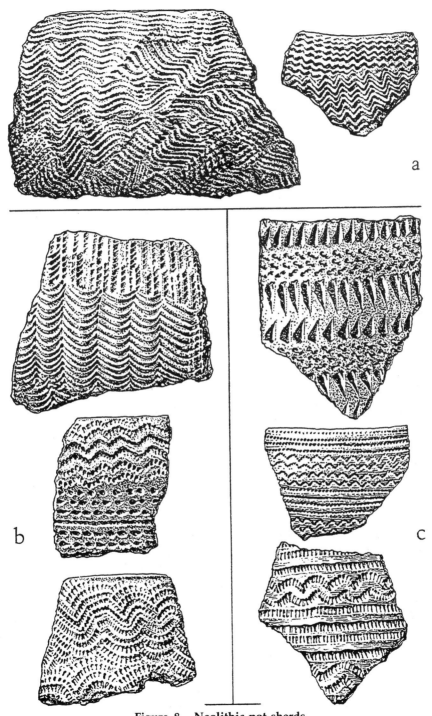

Figure 8. Neolithic pot sherds
(*after* A. J. Arkell, *Early Khartoum*, Oxford, 1949, and *Shaheinab*, Oxford, 1953)

swinderianus). Wild plants will also have been part of the diet. Some burials have been found, within the settlement, all of them in contracted attitudes.

There is no evidence to suggest that the 'Early Khartoum' people had begun to domesticate animals and all the bones found are of wild species – many different ones have been found but the most common are African buffalo (*Syncerus caffer*), kob (*Kobus kob*), warthog (*Phocochoerus aethiopicus*), and hartebeest (*Alcelaphus buselophus*). There is likewise no trace of domesticated plants. The way of life of these people seems little changed from that of those of the Late Upper Palaeolithic except for the significant new addition to technology shown by the making of pottery, and this pottery is well fired and elaborately decorated. It does not look like the efforts of beginners in a new technique but no forerunners have been found. Similar pottery has been found widely distributed across the Sahara, often, though not always, associated with 'Early Khartoum'-type harpoons.

Of the more recently excavated sites of the 'Early Khartoum' people, that at Saggai, 40 kilometres north of Khartoum on the east bank of the Nile, is the best studied and published. The carbon dates show that the site was occupied during the sixth millennium BC and the close resemblance of the material from it (especially the pottery), with that from the Khartoum hospital site serves to date the former site.

The site of Saggai, which seems to have been occupied for about 250–300 years, lay on a lateral bar on the right bank of the ancient course of the Nile. As Arkell had already suggested from evidence at Khartoum Hospital, the climate was considerably moister than it is now and this resulted in the availability of plant food to form a substantial part of the diet. The abundance of sandstone objects, pounders and grinders, is also evidence for the treatment of plant products, though it has been suggested that they had a role in the treatment of meat and also for grinding red ochre, as was also the case at Khartoum. Molluscs were also an important element in the diet, shown by quantities of snail shells, mostly *Pila wernei*, was well as by the high percentage of strontium in the human bones from the site. The excavator (Isabella Caneva) has suggested that the collecting of molluscs and fish, also found in large quantities, was a summertime activity when the Nile flood would have distributed this food resource over a wide stretch of shallow water. Since the only fishing equipment found was the harpoon such conditions would have made fishing much easier by this technique than it would be in the rather fast-flowing main river in winter when the water is at its lowest.

Hunting is indicated by the various mammal remains. Small antelopes predominate amongst these remains, mainly kob (*Kobus kob*) and oribi (*Ourebia ourebi*) and perhaps duiker (*Sylvicapra grimmia*). Since kob would concentrate near the river during the dry season it is suggested that hunting was predominantly a dry season activity.

Table 1 Carbon 14 dates for the Neolithic in Nubia

Early Khartoum

Khartoum Hospital	No dates obtained
Tagra	6420 ± 350 BC
Saggai	6570–5590 BC
	5460 + 100 BC
	5300–100 BC
	5370 ± 100 BC
Shabona	6345–5465 BC
Shaqadud	6190–5375 BC
Sarurab	5615–5090 BC
	7380 ± 110 BC
	7420 ± 110 BC

Shaheinab

Umm Direiwa I	3910–3400 BC
	4690–4135 BC
	5140–4580 BC
Umm Direiwa II	4405–3175 BC
El-Ushara Layer II	3950–3640 BC
Layer III	4420–3880 BC
Islang	5080–4545 BC
Rabak level 2	3500–2915 BC
level 6	5260–4730 BC
level 15	5245–4585 BC
Shaheinab	4815–3685 BC
Kadero I (southern midden)	4395–3800 BC
	4090–3650 BC
	4400–3860 BC
(northern midden)	4530–3995 BC
	4560–4390 BC
	4415–3905 BC
Kadero II	4425–3885 BC
Zakiab	4425–3885 BC
	4725–4385 BC
Nofalab level II	4395–3800 BC
Shaqadud midden	4685–4130 BC

Late Neolithic

El Kedada	3655–3060 BC
	3855–3375 BC
	4325–3828 BC
	3855–3360 BC
	3780–3185 BC
Shaqadud cave level 54	2880–2410 BC
level 38	2970–2410 BC
level 16	2310–1735 BC
level 71	2900–2325 BC

The site of Sarourab 2 almost opposite Saggai on the west bank of the Nile has also produced material comparable with that from the Khartoum Hospital. The stone tools, of which about 70% are of quartz, consist mainly of scrapers, lunates and borers similar to those found at other sites of the period. The pottery is described, though not illustrated, as exhibiting typical 'Early Khartoum' characteristics but some of it is said to be cruder and rougher. Since two of the carbon-14 dates from that site are considerably earlier than from other sites with similar material – about 2,000 years earlier – it may be that Sarourab represents a much earlier development of pottery making but until the pottery is published in detail and more dates are obtained the matter must remain undecided.

Two sites further south, up the White Nile at Tagra and Shabona, also have early dates, though not as early as Sarourab. Shabona, the most fully investigated, 110 kilometres south of Khartoum, is 8 kilometres east of the White Nile on a sandy ridge which at the time of its occupation was a bank of the river. The pottery and the stone tools are closely similar to those from other Early Khartoum sites but study of the pottery shows that there are two types – that with small quartz grains in the clay as temper known as 'Shabona' ware and one with a coarse plant, probably grass, temper called 'Naima' ware. 'Naima' ware is known from Khartoum Hospital but not from Saggai and this suggests that in the area of Khartoum there may have been a boundary between two pottery traditions. Bone harpoon fragments similar to those from Khartoum Hospital also indicate that this site was occupied by people of the same tradition.

These people too were hunters and fishers, and mammal and fish bones were found in quantity, much of it burnt, which implies roasting as a means of preparation. Many bones were fractured to extract the marrow. The largest part of the fauna was fish and tortoise remains, as well as some hippopotamus and crocodile and other river creatures, showing the importance of aquatic resources. The mammals hunted were the same as at other sites of the period including oribi and kob as the most common. The Shabona material confirms the view that the climate of the time was wetter and that there would have been extensive grasslands as well as woodland along the river. It was a favourable environment for a population of hunter gatherers with plentiful food resources from river and plain. Wild plants would also have formed an important part of the diet and the sandstone grinders and pounders which are common at all sites of the period would have been used in processing them. The excavator (J. Desmond Clark) has made an interesting and imaginative attempt to describe the probable conditions of life at the time and supposes that Shabona was a dry-season camp occupied at the time the flood waters were receding. He goes on to say:

Dwellings would have been of reeds plastered with mud. Creeks would have been dammed with fish caught with spears and, possibly, basket traps or simply by reducing oxygen in the water by trampling the mud and so stupefying the fish. Crocodiles and hippos and also elephant were taken from time to time. *Pila* would have been dug out of the mud in to which they had burrowed. As bovines began to collect round the permanent water so hunting in the grassland and *toich* country became more important. Vegetable foods consisted of water plants, cucurbits, fruits and honey collected at the end of the dry season. With the rains, the rise of the Nile and flooding in the *toich* country, the inhabitants of the Shabona base camps would disperse into the hinterland where they would exist by hunting supplemented by using termites and water plants. Most important was the wild grain harvest towards the close of the rains and this would have been collected by the women. Fruits and tubers also became plentiful at this time as the population collected again at Shabona with the onset of the new dry season.

This description relies heavily on modern anthropological observation of those people of the southern Sudan who live in similar environmental conditions, and the term *toich* country refers to the seasonally inundated land along the White Nile and its tributaries which are only swampy during the inundation. During the long dry season there are vast meadows of grass on which the southern Sudanese people, mainly Dinka and Shilluk, feed their large herds of cattle.

Away from the river in Nubia only one site of 'Early Khartoum' times is known, at Shaqadud, in the western Butana about fifty kilometres east of the Nile, where a large site consisting of a cave and a massive midden area were found. Originally discovered by Otto it was re-examined in 1980 by a joint Sudanese and American expedition. There was a long period of occupation at this site (perhaps from c.4000 BC to 1650 BC) and 'wavy line' pottery and stone tools similar to those of the Khartoum Hospital site are present in the early levels and are comparable in date (6190–5375 BC) to other 'Early Khartoum' sites. This evidence shows that the people of the 'Early Khartoum' culture were not restricted to the banks of the river as had seemed likely before the discovery of Shaqadud. Faunal material, though not yet published in detail, shows that the environment was much wetter than today and that rainfall was comparable with that in the Nile valley at the same time. Hunting was important and amongst animals hunted were various types of antelope and even elephants.

Much further north along the Nile in the Dongola reach and immediately south of Wadi Halfa examples of pottery similar to the 'Early Khartoum' have been found. A variety of names define different types but the term 'Khartoum

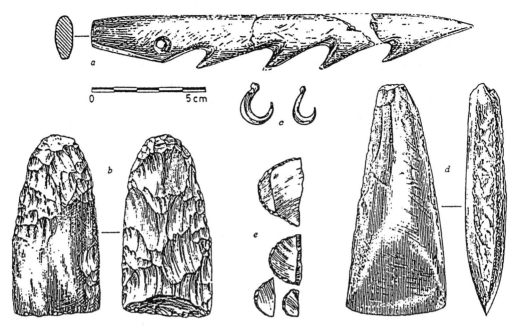

Figure 9.   Artefacts from Shaheinab
(*after* A.J. Arkell, *Shaheinab*, Oxford, 1953)

Variant' covers most of them. Not enough is known to say much about them, but Shiner, who defined the 'Khartoum Variant' industry, says of it, 'There can be little doubt that the Khartoum Variant sites are somehow related to the sites of Early Khartoum and Shaheinab. The ceramics are quite similar and there are parallels in the utilitarian flaked stone tools.'

Although transition from one stage of human development to the next cannot be identified there is no doubt that the material usually known as that of the 'Khartoum Neolithic' is markedly different from that already described. First found, again by Arkell, at Shaheinab, the term 'Khartoum Neolithic' opposed to the rather discredited term 'Khartoum Mesolithic' is confusing since it has not been found at Khartoum. In agreement with normal archaeological terminology it seems better to use the names of the sites where the type material was first found. Thus the earlier culture is here called 'Early Khartoum' and not the 'Khartoum Mesolithic' and the later one 'Shaheinab' and not the 'Khartoum Neolithic'. A number of scholars have objected to the use of Arkell's terms here, but they still continue to be used and continue to cause confusion.

The material culture of the 'Shaheinab' people shows a number of technical advances over that of 'Early Khartoum' and the carbon dates that have now been obtained show it to be later in date and to have flourished from c.4900

BC, that is virtually from the time of the most recent date for 'Early Khartoum' to c.3800 BC and in a later form to c.2700 BC.

The microlithic tools show development from those of 'Early Khartoum' but continue to be made of quartz and to be mainly, as before, lunates, scrapers and engraving tools. In addition to the flaked tools there are found for the first time various polished stone tools of which the diagnostic one is a tool made of rhyolite, a close-grained igneous rock found at the sixth cataract, and usually called a 'gouge' – thought by Arkell, who for a time used 'gouge culture' for what is here called the 'Shaheinab', to have been used for wood working. It has also been suggested that gouges may have been used for digging in the ground. They are very similar to tools found in a Neolithic context in the Fayum in Egypt at about the same date. Other ground stone tools were also found and grindstones made of sandstone were present. These grindstones have often been seen by archaeologists as evidence for the use of cultivated grain, since in later times they were, and still are, used for the grinding of cereal grains. Arkell was very doubtful of their use for grinding grain and pointed out that many of them showed evidence of use for grinding red ochre which he assumed was used as a cosmetic. Even if this was not the sole use for these grindstones they could have been used for grinding the seeds of wild grasses which were widely used as a source of food and still are on occasion in various parts of Africa. It is only the discovery of actual domesticated grains that can show without doubt that agriculture was being practised.

Fish hooks of shell are good evidence for fishing as also are the bone harpoons which are clearly distinguished from those of the earlier 'Early Khartoum' type by having a hole pierced near the base for attaching a line. The presence of beads and other ornaments of amazon stone (microcline feldspar), of carnelian, and lip plugs of zeolite, bone and shell give the impression of a prosperous society. The pottery is very well made with a great variety of patterns made by combing, impressing and incising with various tools, some of shell, others of wood, and much of it is well burnished. This pottery shows all the marks of a sophisticated tradition of expert potters and one of the so far unsolved problems of the archaeology of the period is how such a highly developed pottery could suddenly appear before 4000 BC without any obvious antecedents. Not only is this pottery attractively decorated and well made but it is also found in very great quantity.

A major problem in understanding the life of the people of Nubia in Neolithic times had been to discover the nature of their subsistence and of their housing and social arrangements. For subsistence there is no doubt that hunting, fishing and gathering of vegetable crops still played a part in acquiring food but it is known from a re-study of animal bones from Shaheinab that domestic cattle were present as well as goat or sheep, and since such evidence is present at all the 'Shaheinab' sites that have been investigated it can be said with confidence that the people of the time were keeping domestic animals and were the first people in Nubia to do so. A second study of the Shaheinab material disproves the suggestion that there was a distinct breed of dwarf goat as well as the more usual one, and the evidence suggests just one breed which was similar to the present day Sudanese Nubian goat.

In addition to the original type site of Shaheinab, excavated by Arkell in 1948, a number of other sites of similar date and with similar artefacts are now known (Table 1 lists the main sites with their dates). As a result of this further work a far better picture has now been obtained of the domestic and social life of the time and advances in knowledge have made possible more accurate analyses of faunal and floral materials.

Of these newly found sites (found since the 1970s) several can be described on the basis of partial reports. Although a large number of articles giving preliminary accounts of the work are available none of the sites have yet been published in the detail which Arkell made available within a very short time of the conclusion of the excavations – Khartoum Hospital excavated in 1944, published in 1949, Shaheinab excavated in 1948, published in 1953.

The two largest sites, both on the east bank of the river, are at Kadero and Geili. Both have been excavated since 1972 and work still continues at Kadero where over twenty years have been spent. Other sites are shown on Map 3 and their dates given in Table 1. All these sites contain material closely similar to that from Shaheinab with some variation which implies different activities. Geili, the most completely published, was a much disturbed site heavily dug into for graves in post-Neolithic times. In spite of this disturbance much valuable information was gained and some differences from the 'Shaheinab' assemblage found at Shaheinab has been observed – the pottery is very similar to that of Shaheinab and the flaked stone implements are also closely similar, but they show a much higher percentage of quartz as the raw material (73.1%) compared with other sites of the period and less rhyolite.

The lesser amount of rhyolite used is shown dramatically in the many fewer gouges and this is paralleled by the virtual lack of stone or bone 'celts' or axes which are common at Shaheinab. Presumably this reflects different activities at the two sites – though in view of uncertainty as to the use of the gouges and celts what these activities were cannot be determined. The difference cannot be a reflection of different access to or availability of the raw material, since the sixth cataract from which the rhyolite comes is equally accessible to both sites.

The faunal remains show the presence of domesticated cattle, sheep and goats, not fully recognized in the earlier study of material from Shaheinab, and since domesticated animals have been identified from all the 'Shaheinab' sites it is likely that the people of this period were pastoralists with herds of animals. It has been noted that the Neolithic human bone from Geili shows a higher strontium level than those of Meroitic skeletons from the same site. This suggests that there was a greater dependence on animal food in Neolithic times and strengthens the view that the inhabitants were pastoralists.

Kadero, a little way south of Geili, has also provided much information on the period, though no detailed publication is yet available. It is the largest Neolithic site known in the area with a size of about 30,000 square metres. The artefacts are similar to those from Shaheinab but no fish hooks nor harpoons have been found, and there are very few fish remains. Hunting seems to have played a minor role, but domestic cattle were present – the domestic fauna remains are 80% of the total and show the existence of cattle, sheep, goat and dog. The site may well have been a base site during the rainy season with the inhabitants moving nearer to the river when the rains were over and the river lower. The presence of 55 burials also suggests that Kadero may have been not only a centre for economic activities but also for social ones, and variation in the location of the burials which coincides with different qualities and quantities of grave goods suggests that there were different social classes already in existence.

At one time it was thought that there had been cultivation of domestic sorghum at Kadero from the interpretation of grain impression in potsherds. These impressions are now interpreted as being of wild grasses and there is no certain evidence that grain cultivation was practised, though it has been suggested that wild sorghum may have been deliberately planted, grown and harvested.

The main artefacts at Kadero, pottery and stone, appear to have been generally similar to those from Shaheinab but lack of publication makes it impossible to give a detailed description.

Sites at Zakiab and Umm Direiwa were excavated by Haaland. Zakiab was chosen as being a site close to the river which might show a difference in artefact and food refuse remains which would mark it as being occupied during a different time of year from Kadero. The site is close to what had been an old channel of the river and if it had been occupied during the dry season when the river was low fishing would have been an important source of food. This was found to have been so. Plenty of fish bones, mostly lung fish (*Protopterus sp.*) which composed 72% of the fish remains, as well as molluscs of which the swamp snail *Pila* was the dominant type, were present and fish hooks of shell and bone harpoons similar to those from Shaheinab were found.

The stone tools were similar to those from Kadero but the number of grindstones was much less, whilst scrapers, probably for treating hides, were common. The large quantity of stone waste suggests that the site was one where production of stone tools was an important activity. The fact that there were burials at Kadero but not at the other nearby sites also supports the suggestion that Kadero was a base site and a central gathering ground for people who at some times of year, probably the dry winter season, dispersed more widely to settle in smaller communities.

Umm Direiwa, another rather large site of about 9,000 square metres, lies seven kilometres from the Nile. It much resembles Kadero with many cattle bones and some of sheep and goat but no sign of fishing and very few fish remains, as befits a site so far from the river. Artefacts of pottery and stone follow the normal 'Shaheinab' styles and gouges were very common, as were grinding stones. The significance of the proportion of stone objects is not understood but Haaland, assuming that the grindstones were for food production, probably for grinding wild cereals, has supposed the gouges were for digging in the ground, though she may have been influenced by the assumed identification of domesticated grain at Kadero into thinking that sorghum was being grown both at Kadero and Umm Direiwa.

A number of other sites of the period are known close to the river bank on the west side at Ushara, Nofalab and Islang, all of which produced similar material and dates which are comparable with those of other 'Shaheinab' sites.

The site of Shaqadud, already mentioned as being occupied in 'Early Khartoum' times, is not only noteworthy for being away from the river but it is one of only two sites – the other being Qoz, a small badly eroded site found by Arkell – which show the two early ceramic cultures of the central Nile valley in a clear stratigraphic relationship. In the Shaqadud midden at about 1.50 metres below the surface in the words of the excavator 'there are the first hints of a shift from Khartoum Mesolithic ("Early Khartoum") assemblage types toward one that might be considered Khartoum Neolithic ("Shaheinab"). This is not seen in the lithic materials which show a depressing consistency in their poor workmanship, the poverty of the forms involved, and in the general paucity of retouched tools. Rather, this tendency is seen in the ceramics.'

There is no clear dividing line between the two styles of ceramics though the excavator suggests, on the basis of carbon dates, that the change was happening at about 3,500 BC which is rather later than the dates for the beginning of the 'Shaheinab' style from other sites. There are some clear differences between the 'Shaheinab' period at Shaqadud and at contemporary sites in the Nile valley. Of these the most striking is the absence of domestic animals which are attested at all of the river side sites of the period. The other difference is the absence of rhyolite gouges – the diagnostic artefact at other sites – and the almost total absence of rhyolite as a tool-making material, and of bone axes, amazonite beads and zeolite lip plugs, all normally found in sites of the period. In addition, as would be expected in a site so far from the river, there is none of the equipment used for fishing – fish hooks, harpoons and net weights. The evidence suggests that though not entirely out of contact with the dwellers along the Nile, as the similarity in ceramics suggests, the inhabitants of Shaqadud had a different life style adapted to the grasslands of the Butana and were largely dependent for their food supplies on the wild animals and vegetation to be found there. At least during the earlier occupation of the site with the increased rainfall there would have been many wooded areas suitable for the game that they were hunting.

A recent study of the pottery and its decoration from this site suggests strong cultural influences from the Sahara and implies that much of the cultural development at Shaqadud was not closely related to that of the Nile Valley.

In Nubia a major archaeological problem has been the lack of any sites or artefacts from the period of the apparent end of the 'Shaheinab' in the early fourth millennium BC to the first settlements in Meroitic times early in the first millennium BC (see chapter 6 for Meroe), a gap of some 2,000 years for which no evidence of human activity was visible. Dates from Shaqadud of the third millennium have done something to close the gap, at least away from the river, and the site of Kedada has provided dates of the late fourth millennium from what might be called a 'Late Neolithic' period.

At Kedada there is evidence for a distinct development with pottery similar to that from two graves found at Omdurman Bridge by Arkell and from some graves from Geili. This group of sites has well made pottery with different shapes and decorative techniques from the impressed and incised wares of earlier Neolithic settlements. Much of the pottery is decorated by rippling, a technique common in Nubia during the A-Group (see chapter 3) and also known from Egypt. In addition to the pottery, polished stone palettes for grinding cosmetics, clay female figurines, various bone artefacts such as harpoons, a hair comb and a spoon were found. The variety and craftsmanship of the finds suggests a richer society than earlier ones and the presence of Red Sea shells shows that there was external contact. The evidence of domestic cattle, sheep and goats is more plentiful than for the earlier 'Shaheinab' people and it is suggested that the increase of domestication and the lessening of hunting as a means of subsistence may indicate some change in the environment with a decrease in rainfall.

Arkell had already realized from his finds at Omdurman Bridge that there was material post-dating that from Shaheinab and he suggested that this was due to A-Group refugees fleeing from early pharaonic Egyptian attacks in Lower Nubia. This is a rather fanciful suggestion and it seems more likely that there was a common, or at least a related, culture throughout the Nubian

Nile valley and for the present the term 'Late Neolithic' seems suitable for these manifestations and the late ones from Shaqadud.

Although the area of Nubia close to the junction of the Niles, the sites of which have just been described, is the best studied, some information about the period was obtained in the northern area where most of the Old Stone Age studies were made. Several different ceramic styles were identified, though the eroded nature of the sites made more detailed information difficult to obtain and there is none of the now rather abundant material for understanding economic and social life which has been obtained in the Khartoum region.

The final stages of the stone age investigated during the Aswan dam salvage campaign identified three different ceramic traditions, the post-Shamarkian, the 'Khartoum Variant' and the Abkan. These have been grouped together with the Nubian A-Group (in this book dealt with in a separate chapter) under the term Early Nubian. All the sites explored were badly eroded and only ceramic sherds and stone artefacts were available to define the different traditions. The 'Khartoum Variant' appears to be the oldest and the ceramics resemble the late 'Early Khartoum' type known as 'Dotted Wavy Line' from its decorative patterns which represent a later development from the 'Wavy Line' well known from the Khartoum Hospital and other contemporary sites. No dates have been obtained from the 'Khartoum Variant' in Nubia but discoveries in the Egyptian Sahara have revealed sites with 'Early Khartoum' pottery and with stone tools similar to those of the 'Khartoum Variant'. The oldest is dated to c.6000 ± 100 BC and the latest to c.5200 BC.

Of the post-Shamarkian little is known, the main site only producing 171 pot sherds. For the Abkan considerably more is known and carbon dates place it late in the fourth millennium BC and approximately contemporary with the Shaheinab.

The technology and typology of the Abkan stone tools suggest a link between those of the Qadan and the Abkan, the most common tools being borers and groovers. The Abkan pottery is quite different from that of the Khartoum variant with its clear connection with the Khartoum area ceramics. It is plain and undecorated and one ware is, in the words of Nordström, who has worked extensively in the area, 'the earliest in the great array of burnished or polished hand-made wares developed in Nubia.' There is also some pottery with a rippled surface, fore-runner of the characteristic rippled ware of the A-Group.

The type site of the Abkan is of special interest because an excavation was made there with the intention of co-relating the artefact material with the rock drawings. Rock drawings are common throughout the second cataract and adjacent areas and a special study of them was made by the Scandinavian Joint Expedition to Sudanese Nubia. The drawings cover a long range of date

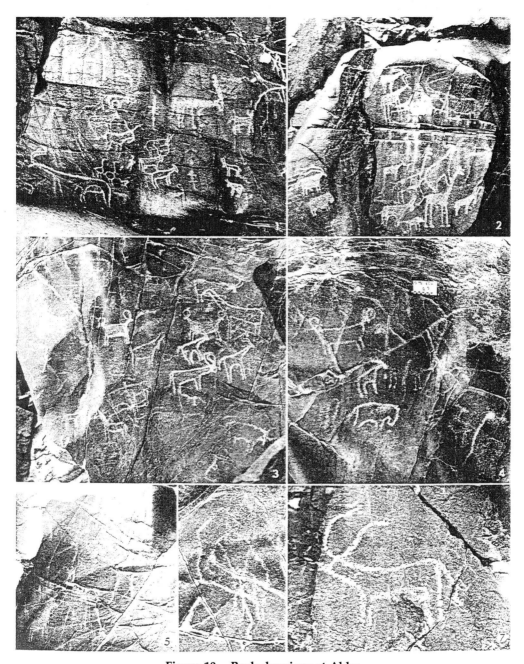

Figure 10.   Rock drawings at Abka
(*from* H. A. Nordstrom, *Scandinavian Joint Expedition to Sudanese Nubia*, vol. 3.2, Uppsala, 1972; courtesy
of Professor Säve-Söderbergh)

but some certainly seem to be associated with sites of the early ceramic cultures of Nubia.

The climate of the time, as is the case further south, was more favourable than it became later and there was a savanna type of vegetation with acacia and other trees and much grass which supported herbivorous animals such as elephant, hippopotamus and wild cattle.

Very little information is available to fill the large geographical gap between the now rather well known Neolithic of the central Sudan in the region of the confluence of the Blue and White Niles and the scantier remains in the second cataract area, but one survey was carried out in the Dongola reach by a team from Southern Methodist University. Four groups of ceramics were differentiated of which the first, and presumably earliest, was called the 'Early Khartoum Related Group'. Pottery of this group is similar to that of 'Early Khartoum' with 'wavy line' and 'dotted wavy line' sherds. The stone tools are mainly microliths and lunates are common. The second group, the 'Karat Group', differs markedly and pottery decoration resembles that of 'Shaheinab'. Stone tools are also mainly microlithic and rhyolite gouges, characteristic of 'Shaheinab', were not found.

The 'Tergis Group' and the 'El Malik Group' were less clearly differentiated and the pottery is less well known, though most of it is red slipped. The very preliminary nature of the Dongola reach survey shows that at least the ceramic types known from the central Sudan were in use there, implying a wide area with a common culture.

CHAPTER 3

THE A-GROUP AND FIRST CONTACTS WITH EGYPT

◆

At about the same time as the beginning of recorded Egyptian history, a little before 3000 BC, a distinctive culture appears in Lower Nubia which has been known since its first identification in 1907 by Reisner as the A-Group. The name was given when the Archaeological Survey of Nubia, called into being by the first heightening of the Aswan dam in the years 1908–10, began its work.

In surveying an area that was virtually unknown archaeologically, Reisner, the director of the survey, found material remains of various peoples whose artefacts were very different from Egyptian ones, it was not possible to use a terminology appropriate to Egypt to identify them, so Reisner devised a simple code, using letters of the alphabet for all the cultures which could not be identified with those of Egypt. The earliest one that he identified was therefore named the A-Group. Further letters of the alphabet were used for later archaeological entities when there was no obvious Egyptian or other historical period with which the new material could be associated. Reisner defined a B-Group, now no longer considered to be a separate culture and discussed below, a C-Group and then towards the end of the period he was studying, since there was a long chronological gap which might produce archaeological material previously unknown, an X-Group. These different groups will be described and discussed in their proper places. Several authors have suggested new terminologies to replace the 'Groups' of Reisner but the original terms are so widely used in the relevant literature that it seems more convenient to retain them so long as it is realized that they are only a useful and easy way to label peoples for whom we have no better name.

The people whom we know as the A-Group were certainly in touch with those of late pre-dynastic and early dynastic times in Egypt, though there are sufficient differences in artefacts and in other cultural features to make it reasonably certain that the A-Group does not represent an incursion by Egyptians into Nubia, as used to be thought. Reisner, for example, not having found evidence, or perhaps not having looked for it, for a Late Stone Age occupation, now well known and described in the previous chapter, assumed that Lower Nubia was an empty land and that the A-Group represented the incursion of a pre-dynastic Egyptian population into the area. Now that we know of earlier inhabitants and can see some continuity with the Abkan, Qadan and Khartoum Variant cultures of earlier times we can be sure that this earlier interpretation was wrong and the A-Group peoples were indigenous and the descendants of a population that had been in the area for hundreds or even thousands of years.

There was certainly close contact with Egypt and it is the finding of characteristic and well known Egyptian objects in A-Group graves that has made it possible to date the culture and to define different periods during which there were changes in the indigenous Nubian material. These periods have been named Early, Classic and Terminal and the dates given to them depend mainly on cross-dating made possible by the presence of a considerable number of Egyptian objects of known dates in A-Group contexts, mainly in graves and consisting largely of pottery.

The Early A-Group can be chronologically equated with the Naqada I and II periods of the Egyptian pre-dynastic period and can be dated to about 4000 to 3500 BC, with the Classic to about 3500 BC and the Terminal at the beginning of the First Dynasty of Egypt which is dated with reasonable certainty to about 3200 BC. These dates have been mainly arrived at by laboratory testing of organic materials, mostly charcoal, to provide carbon-14 dates. For prehistoric times that is not only the most reliable method of dating but frequently the only one, apart from intelligent guesses. By the beginning of the First Dynasty of Egypt we are approaching a period for which there are written documents which provide some historical details and also make it possible to establish dates by conventional historical methods. By making calculations based on knowledge of many Egyptian Pharaohs and the length of their reigns a very similar date had been arrived at for the beginning of the Egyptian monarchy and c.3200 BC is generally accepted for this event. From Egyptian objects in A-Group tombs this date for the flourishing of the Terminal A-Group cannot be far wrong.

Present research suggests, in the words of Adams, that the A-Group was a 'localised, peripheral Egyptian culture' in the sense of peripheral to Egypt; this does not imply that the inhabitants of Nubia were ethnically the same as pre- and proto-dynastic Egyptians. Adams's phrase indicates correctly that the A-Group is only found in the area of Nubia closest to Egypt, that is Lower Nubia, and so far no traces of it have been found up stream of the second cataract. The most northerly site known is at Kubania, 10 kilometres

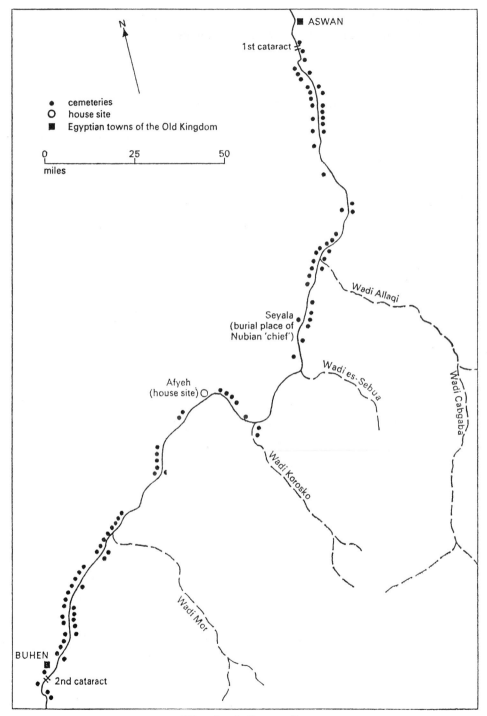

Map 4. A-Group sites

north of Aswan, and the furthest south is close to Saras in the southern fringes of the second cataract. The A-Group is essentially a culture of Lower Nubia and its contemporaries further south would seem to be the people whose life and material objects have been described in the previous chapter.

The increasing number of sites of this period suggests an increase in population, though it still cannot have been very large, and no single settlement will have had more than a few dozen inhabitants, with even the bigger ones probably containing less than a hundred. It has been estimated that the total population of Lower Nubia in A-Group times was no more than 8,000, though some would put it at less. It is very difficult to make estimates of ancient populations but since the region has been surveyed so many times it is probably archaeologically the most intensively studied stretch of country in the world – and since it is restricted to the Nile valley it is unlikely that many sites, other than very small ones, have been overlooked, so that by calculating the number of dwelling sites – over forty have been found – and cemeteries, a reasonable judgement can be made.

This increase of population is likely to be closely related to the beginning of agriculture. The finding of grains of wheat and barley and peas and lentils attests to the cultivation of domesticated crops and suggests that the A-Group people were the first to practise agriculture in this part of the Nile valley, using the Nile flood plain which, inundated and fertilised with fresh silt every year, provided excellent opportunities for the growing of crops. Evidence for the keeping of domestic animals is less certain and only a very few bones that may come from goat and cattle have been found. Hunting, shown by the finding of gazelle bones, the collecting of wild plants and fishing continued to be an important element in the food supply. Copper fish hooks, from Egypt, are first found at this time and are good evidence for the use of fish in the diet.

The finding of more permanent housing than is known from earlier times is another indication, along with the beginning of crop growing, that with the A-Group we have the first permanent settlements. Many settlements of this period, defined by a surface scatter of characteristic pot sherds, sometimes other objects and hearths, have a lack of any obvious building structures and this makes it likely that these dwellings consisted of straw and reed huts. At a few sites more permanent structures have been found; of these the most important was at Afia where remains of dry stone built houses were found, one of which contained at least six rooms. The floors of these rooms were of mud and pebbles. The site at Afia is the most extensive A-Group village found but a few permanent stone built houses have been found at other places.

In addition to small villages in the open some A-Group people were living in rock shelters where these were available, one at Sayala being especially

1a. View of the Nile

1b. View of Nile with ruins on an island

2. Saquia Wheel

3. Nubian woman

4a. Well in Bayuda desert

4b. Camel in Bayuda desert

5a and 5b. A group pots

6. A Group pots

7a. A Group burial

7b. A Group clay figurines

8a. C group pots

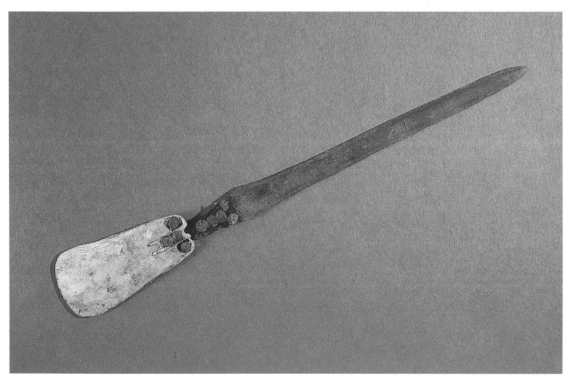

8b. Kerma period knife

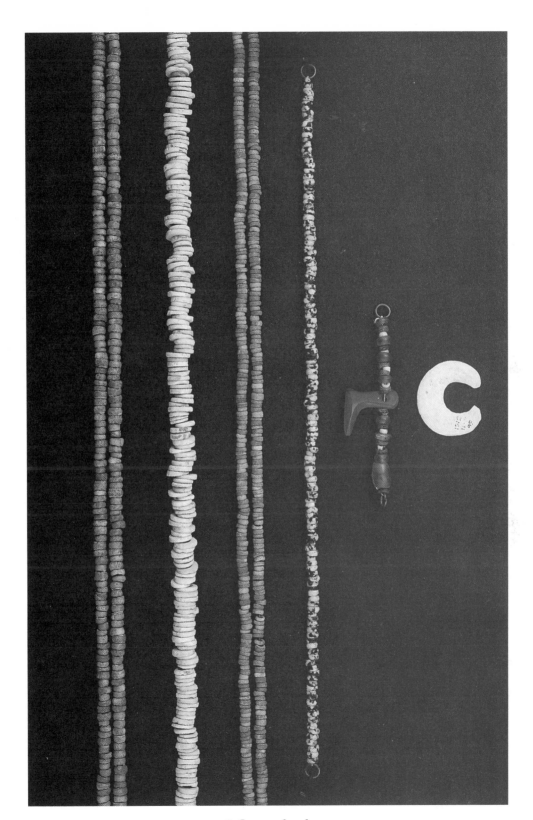

9. C group beads

10a. Kerma West Deffufa

10b. Kerma East Deffufa

11a. Kerma pots

11b. Kerma burial

12a. C-Group cemetery at Ashkeit

12b. Tumulus grave at Kerma

13. Statue of Senuwy

14a. The Semna cararact

14b. Uronarti

15. Pharaonic statue at Tombos

16a. Gubbat el Hawa, Aswan

16b. Elephantine island

17a. Fort at Sai island

17b. Temple of Tuthmosis III at Semna

18a. Soleb temple

18b. Gebel Barkal

19a. Abu Simbel temple

19b. Nubian prisoners, Abu Simbel

20a. Buhen fort

20b. Buhen fort

21a. Amara West town wall

21b. Amara West town street

22. Soleb temple

23. Barkal temple from top of the hill

24a. Pyramid of Taharqa at Nuri

24b. Nuri pyramids

25a. Air view of Meroe town

25b. The Lion temple at Naqa

26a. Meroe pyramids

26b. Air view of Meroe pyramids

27. Meroe excavations

28a. Axumite inscription from Meroe

28b. Tabo temple

29a. Old Dongola church

29b. Church of the Columns at Old Dongola

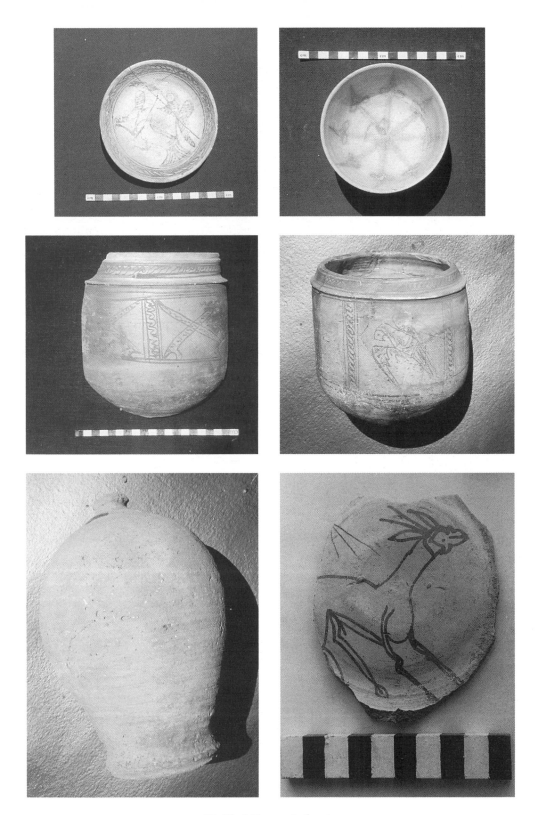

30. Christian period pots

31a. Mograka church

31b. Debeira West house

32a. Wooden figure of St Michael from Attiri

32b. Christian tombstone inscribed in Greek

complex with some wall constructions and with rock drawings which may be contemporary. In addition to these various types of domestic dwellings there were several sites in which no houses or huts were found. There were many storage pits containing pottery vessels – the largest of these was at Sheikh Daud where 578 such pits were found. At this site there is no indication of human occupation nor of fire places, but the large number of pits, most of which contained pottery of late pre-dynastic Egyptian type, together with flint tools and grains of barley and wheat, show that some important activity had taken place here.

If it is correct that there are no dwellings at Sheikh Daud then an explanation is required for the existence of large-scale storage facilities at a place without permanent inhabitants. It has been suggested that the site was one to which people came to barter goods and the heavy preponderance of Egyptian pottery and the lack of typical A-Group pottery has led to the suggestion that it was important for the exchange of Egyptian goods for the products of Nubia. The excavator's proposal that the site was for large-scale dairy production has not been accepted by most scholars and it has been pointed out that there is very little evidence in the form of identified bones for the large herds of cattle that would be required for such activity. However the large amount of animal, probably cattle, dung used as temper in much of the clay used for pottery implies that there were cattle in some areas. It has been suggested that cattle were not herded in large numbers by A-Group people but that there were pastoral people living nearby who were the cattlekeepers and that there was a symbiotic relationship between nomadic pastoralists whose tenuous archaeological remains have not been found, and the settled A-Group.

The most distinctive product of A-Group times is the indigenous Nubian pottery and it is largely by its presence that assemblages of this period can be identified. There are several different types of pottery found of which the primary division is between the native Nubian wares and the imported Egyptian ones. Some of the Nubian pottery is extremely fine – a so-called 'egg-shell' ware burnished and painted in various patterns, mainly a series of triangles in dark red paint – but there are also several other types and a variety of shapes. Although the 'egg-shell' ware, which seems not to have existed prior to the time of the Terminal A-Group, is the best known because of its unique style of decoration, more of the pottery consists of bowls of a bright red burnished and rippled exterior, frequently with black rims as in much Egyptian pottery of the same time, though the Nubian pottery is not identical with that from Egypt and can be distinguished from it. Since there was, on the evidence of many imported Egyptian objects, close contact with pre-dynastic Egypt it seems likely that the idea of blackening the mouths of pottery vessels in this way came from Egypt, though it is noticeable that although this style of decoration disappeared from Egyptian pottery at the very beginning of dynastic times it continued for several centuries in Nubia. The method by which the black rims were obtained was by placing the pots, after firing, rims down in a smouldering pile of the fuel used in the original firing until the interior and the rim became black leaving the rest of the vessel red (Plates 5a, 5b, 6).

The imported Egyptian pottery was of types well known from late predynastic Egypt. These pots, mainly jars and open bowls, are assumed not to have come from Egypt empty, as pottery trade items, but to have been filled with food and drink products not available in Nubia, such as wine, beer, cheese and oil. No direct evidence for these products had been found and beer in particular is most unlikely to have been transported over any long distance. Since the Nubians were growing barley it is improbable that they could not make the beer they needed for local consumption. The suggestion that Egyptian pots were being used for the import of food and drink is a reasonable one since it seems unlikely that a people with an advanced ceramic tradition of their own would have needed to import the very large quantities of Egyptian pottery that have been found, except as containers. If used as containers the jars would have had to be sealed and a few such mud sealings have been found, some examples having impressed designs.

TOOLS AND UTENSILS

Although there is a similarity between the flaked stone tools of the A-Group and the preceding Abkan ones there is a deterioration in the stone-working technology of the A-Group, and the introduction of copper tools, certainly imported from Egypt, shows a change from a complete reliance on stone as a material for tools and weapons.

Grinding stones are common but it need not be assumed that they were only used for grinding domesticated grain – wild grains also need grinding, as has been suggested in the previous chapter. Stone mace heads, also likely to have been imported from Egypt, have been found, two from Sayala having gold-plated handles and depictions of animals in a style closely resembling some forms from pre-dynastic Egypt. The copper tools found include axe heads, adzes, chisels, knife blades and many small pointed tools which may be needles or awls. No trace of copper working has been found at A-Group sites so it seems likely that all these tools are also imports.

Some small tools, borers or awls, of bone are known, as also are items of ivory, of which spoons, though not common, are the most usual. Other objects are beads of ostrich egg shell, common at all periods in the ancient Sudan, semi-precious stones of various types of quartz of which carnelian is the most

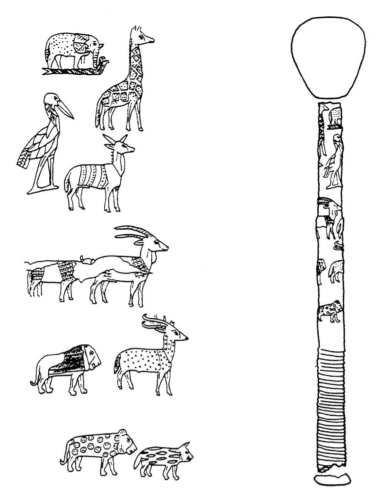

Figure 11. Gold-handled mace of the A-Group
(*after* C. M. Firth, *Archaeological Survey of Nubia*, Cairo, 1908–9)

common, faience and at least one of gold. Pendant amulets of shell, ivory, bone and faience are also numerous in burials.

Representations of the human form are known only from clay female figurines. Two were found by the Scandinavian expedition at their site 227 at Halfa Degheim and a few elsewhere in Nubia.

BURIALS

The vast majority of sites of the A-Group are cemeteries. Over 3,000 graves have been excavated, and most of what we know about the people is obtained from their burials. A-Group times provide the first appearance of organized cemeteries and over one hundred are known. Most of them average about fifty graves though a few are considerably larger.

Two types of graves are known. One, the most common, consists of an oval pit usually about 80 centimetres deep, though perhaps originally somewhat deeper since there has been much surface erosion over the whole area of Nubia and the original surface has been removed (Plate 7a). A second, rarer, type of grave consists of a pit similar to that of the first type with a lateral niche for the body dug out at one side. This is the first appearance of a grave type which was to continue until Meroitic times. The bodies were buried in a contracted position, lying on the right side and usually facing south. Some were laid on reed mats and wrapped in leather. The graves always contained a number of grave goods – pottery, items of personal adornment and utensils of daily use. One exceptionally rich cemetery at Sayala had larger graves than the normal. These graves were of the ordinary pit type but larger and roofed with sandstone slabs. The grave contents were also richer than usual and not only contained the two maces with gold plate on the handles already mentioned but also a number of copper axes, ingots and other tools of copper, two large slate palettes and other material suggesting the interment of somebody of wealth and importance, perhaps a chief. This cemetery is perhaps the earliest evidence for social stratification to be found in Nubia. Studies of skeletal remains, of which many have been recovered, show the average height for men to have been 169.9 centimetres and 155.5 for women. They do not seem to have been physically different from their contemporaries in Upper Egypt, and some well preserved bodies show that they had black or dark brown hair, usually straight.

During recent years there has been some discussion arising from a startling suggestion made by Bruce Williams based on the results of excavations at Qustul. Here an expedition from the University of Chicago excavated in the 1960s as part of the Aswan dam salvage project and found an A-Group cemetery consisting of eight graves considerably larger than usual and twenty-five of the normal A-Group type. The suggestion has been made that these large graves represent the burial places of a very early line of kings pre-dating the first dynasty of Egypt and being perhaps its precursor. The evidence for this is very slight and has not won general approval. It is based on the assumption that the size of the tombs and their contents are such that they must be considered 'royal'. In addition to this there are several objects, said to be from tombs, which bear designs of royal significance. There are three pottery vessels, certainly of Egyptian manufacture, but claimed to have been decorated locally, and one or more incense burners, one at least of which has in sunk relief a representation of boats and a pharaonic icon in the form of a figure wearing the crown of Upper Egypt. The depiction of royal emblems on these objects is established; what is not certain is whether they were imported from Egypt, in which case they cannot be used as an argument for a local Nubian origin of Egyptian royalty. If they are genuinely indigenous to Nubia then they can be used to suggest not, perhaps, a Nubian origin for Egypt's first dynasty but at least that the A-Group were aware of the emblems used by the ruler of Upper Egypt, and also perhaps that the A-Group had already developed a system of rule by powerful chiefs. A discussion as to whether those buried in the Qustul graves were 'royal' or only 'chiefs' seems overly concerned with modern terminology for rulers. The author of this suggestion claims that the large graves at Qustul, known to the excavators as cemetery L, each represent a single royal generation and that the grave containing the finest of the incense burners is to be dated to 'six or seven generations before the start of the first dynasty (of Egypt)', that is to say to about 3,400 BC.

Evidence of Egyptian contact with the A-Group in Nubia is certain enough from the amount of Egyptian material found in the cemeteries but it is less certain what the nature of the contact was, though commercial contacts and exchange of goods was, without doubt, part of it. There is nothing from Egypt to throw direct light on the problem, but a rock carving from Gebel Sheikh Suleiman near Wadi Halfa and now removed to the National Museum in Khartoum may provide some information on Egyptian activities in Nubia early in the first dynasty. The scene is generally taken to represent an Egyptian military incursion into Nubia. It shows a prisoner tied to a typically Egyptian ship with corpses lying, presumably in the water, below the ship. Another bound prisoner seems to have a bow, an Egyptian symbol for a part of Nubia, attached to him and is therefore, perhaps, a Nubian prisoner. Two signs are shown standing on the hieroglyph for a town and indicate either captured towns or the region in which the campaign took place. Usually considered to be of the time of King Djer, though some have doubted this and think that no royal name is written, there is little doubt that the relief is Egyptian and dates from early in the first dynasty and therefore indicates some pharaonic military activity at least as far as the down-stream end of the second cataract.

It also seems likely that the Egyptians were trading in Nubia, as in later times, not for artefacts – virtually no A-Group objects have been found in Egypt – but for the luxury raw materials some of which Nubia could provide. Nubia could also give access to regions further south. Such items as gold, leopard skins, giraffe tails, ebony and particularly ivory led the Egyptians in pharaonic times to push further into Nubia, as described in chapter 4. The most southerly Egyptian inscriptions of the Old Kingdom so far known were

Figure 12. Relief of King Djer near Wadi Halfa
(*after* A. J. Arkell, *Journal of Egyptian Archaeology*, vol. 36, 1950)

found at Kulb and refer to a 'scribe of the prospectors'. This strongly suggests that as with many early Egyptian penetrations to the south the aim was to look for minerals or high quality stone for sculpture or building.

The later stages of A-Group times – the Terminal A-Group – were the richest. The number of settlements increased, suggesting a growth of population, and richer imported Egyptian objects are found in the graves such as the gold-handled maces from Sayala, already referred to, and which it has been suggested were rewards to a Nubian chief for supplying mercenaries to serve the king of Egypt.

It is noticeable that no Egyptian goods later than the early years of the first dynasty of Egypt are found in A-Group sites and the evidence seems to point to a rather sudden de-population of Lower Nubia, reasons for which are not well understood. There may have been a lessening of the amount of agricultural land, caused by a drop in river level and resulting in a reduction in the population, or an emigration north and south, but archaeological evidence does not support this interpretation. Whatever happened it seems clear that the Nubian material characteristic of the A-Group had a rather short life and disappeared from archaeological view soon after 3000 BC.

It had been suggested by Reisner that a number of poor graves, poor that is in grave goods, represented the late survival of the A-Group and survived through the Egyptian Old Kingdom, filling the gap between the observed end of the A-Group and the beginning of the C-Group. He used the term B-Group, implying that this group came chronologically after the A-Group. A detailed study made in the 1960s has shown conclusively that the original dating of these graves was wrong and they all belong to A-Group times, though they are much poorer, or in some cases more fully robbed, than other A-Group graves. This study has demonstrated that there was a greater range in the wealth shown by grave contents than had been previously realized and emphasizes that there was a considerable social and economic differentiation amongst the A-Group people.

Adams has argued cogently that the several centuries without any cultural material is an illusion and that it is likely that the A-Group lasted much later than is usually assumed. The difficulty with this argument, though common sense would suggest that it has merit, is that material of the Egyptian Old Kingdom later than the first dynasty is not found in A-Group contexts.

CHAPTER 4

THE C-GROUP, KERMA AND THE BEGINNINGS OF URBAN LIFE

———————◆———————

The next distinct archaeological entity from Nubia is that known as the C-Group. The people of this culture were spread throughout Lower Nubia through virtually the same region as their predecessors, the A-Group, and the culture lasted from about 2250 BC at the end of the Egyptian Old Kingdom through the First Intermediate period and lasted well into the Egyptian Middle Kingdom some time after 2000 BC. The whole period of the C-Group has been divided by Bietak, who has made a detailed chronological study, into various periods which he has called Ia and Ib which correspond to about 2200–1950 BC, the period of the very end of the Egyptian Old Kingdom through the First Intermediate period to the beginning of the Middle Kingdom; IIa and IIb from about 1950 to 1600 BC, equivalent to the Middle Kingdom and the early part of the Second Intermediate period; and III which corresponds to the latter part of the Second Intermediate and apparently lasted to the beginning of the eighteenth dynasty and the New Kingdom in 1500 BC.

The C-Group shows a number of cultural characteristics in common with the A-Group as well as occupying the same territory, although their very distinctive black pottery with incised, and often white-filled, decoration is quite different from any earlier ceramics and will be a recurrent pottery type in the Sudan for a long period, occurring again in Meroitic times as late as the first few centuries AD.

The common thread of culture between the A- and the C-Groups, although they seem to be separated by a long period of time (several hundred years), makes an interpretation of events difficult. As was described in the last chapter, traces of the A-Group, whose chronology is well defined by the Egyptian objects found in their sites, disappear at some time early in the Egyptian first dynasty and no Nubian material can be identified during the period of the Old Kingdom until the earliest C-Group sites which appear to be contemporary with the sixth dynasty.

There has been much discussion of the origins of this Nubian C-Group and some have suggested that they came from the western desert as nomadic pastoralists forced to move into the Nile valley by the gradual desiccation of the once fertile desert. Others have suggested an eastern origin, and pottery similar to that of the C-Group has been found in the Red Sea region as well as at Agordat in Eritrea. Pottery with resemblances to that of both the A- and C-Groups has also been found as far south as Omdurman at the junction of the Blue and White Niles.

Consideration of the very close similarities in the artefacts of the A- and C-Groups, in burial customs, and in the close physical resemblance, which study of skeletons suggests, makes it much more likely that these inhabitants of Nubia were fundamentally the same people as their predecessors of the A-Group and that the changes, which are mainly seen in increasing sophistication of the pottery, increased elaboration of burial customs and of the objects, frequently Egyptian, which were contained in the graves, were due to normal development during the passing of time and the introduction of new material from Egypt. Some scholars strongly disagree and see the C-Group people as being a different people who moved into Nubia from west or south.

It is a more economical explanation of the occupation of Nubia in C-Group times to suggest that these people were descendants of those of earlier times, the Neolithic and A-Group people, who were their forerunners. A view of Nubian history which stresses the continuity of culture and population is more in keeping with the archaeological evidence than is one which requires large-scale immigration. It may be that part of Nubia was abandoned early in the old Kingdom at the end of A-Group times, about 2800 BC or even a little earlier until about 2200 BC when the first C-Group occupation can be identified.

If it is correct that most of Lower Nubia was largely abandoned for about six hundred years – and, unlikely though that seems, it is indicated by the lack of archaeological evidence for that period – then it seems that the Nubians had moved out of Lower Nubia proper, perhaps to the south, and then returned when conditions changed and made living there once more possible. These moves, if this interpretation is correct, may have been in response to changes in river level which controlled the amount of land available for agriculture. Certainly by about 2200 BC the area was once more occupied and there was an increase of population. It has been estimated that it may have been of the order of 17,000 by the end of the period though it seems to have been considerably less in earlier times.

As is usual, most of the information about these people comes from their cemeteries which are widely distributed throughout Lower Nubia. The burial styles are similar to those of the A-Group though somewhat more elaborate, particularly the late ones, and the grave contents are richer. The cemeteries are usually larger than those of the A-Group as the suggested increase in population would require.

Graves of the Ia and Ib periods were round or oval pits in the sandy soil and bodies were laid in a flexed position with face usually pointing north and head to the east. The grave superstructure consisted of a circular dry stone wall about 1 metre high and sometimes as much as 5 metres in diameter, filled with sand and gravel. In addition a range of objects were placed with the burial, and pots, which almost certainly contained food offerings, a custom still current in Nubia, were placed against the outside of the superstructure, normally on the east side. Some graves had stone slabs, resembling grave stones, often carved with depictions of cattle, placed beside them.

In the later period (IIa onward) the graves were more frequently rectangular, sometimes lined or roofed with stone slabs, and the superstructures, still built in the same way, were broader and lower. Towards the end of C-Group times some graves consisted of a pit lined with sun-dried mud bricks and roofed with a brick vault and were as much as 16 metres in diameter. Several had rectangular sun-dried brick buildings, almost certainly chapels, where offerings to the dead could be placed against the graves.

The dwellings of the living are not as well known nor as easily identifiable as are the cemeteries but there is some evidence for them. One of the earliest sites was found at Sayala West where there is an oval enclosure of stone, probably built as a base on which to erect a less substantial wall of reeds or thorn bush, and which is 25 metres in diameter. Within this enclosure wall are the remains of similar but smaller structures, also roughly circular, which mark the positions of huts. This suggests the residence of more than a nuclear family, perhaps an extended family, all living closely together but each unit having its own hut. Trigger has suggested, using ethnographic examples, that this settlement may have been lived in by a man, his several wives and their children. This is an interesting speculation and fits the observable evidence but it is not one susceptible to proof by archaeological means. At another site, Aniba, it seems that people were living in tents since not only was the hole for the central post found but also holes for smaller posts forming a circle 4 to 5 metres in diameter. This is not incontrovertible proof that the dwellings were tents since the posts may have been for a circular hut, but since fragments of leather which could have been the tent covering were found it is a possible interpretation.

Aniba is an exceptionally interesting and important site because it has different periods of occupation superimposed on each other. The earliest one consists of the tented settlement already described. Above it were found round houses partly dug into the ground, and with at least the lower parts of the walls made of upright stone slabs. The construction of the upper part of the walls and of the roof is not known, though like the Sayala houses they are likely to have been made of light branches or reeds and the roofs would have been thatched. Above these were buildings consisting of rectangular rooms built of sun-dried bricks, a building technique which may have been introduced by Egyptians. Of one such building found at Debeira East the excavator said that had it not been for the C-Group pottery found in it the building would have been taken for an Egyptian one. This is a good example of how far Egyptian influence had gone by the later C-Group period.

In very late C-Group times, during the Egyptian Second Intermediate period, there is seen to be an increase in the size of settlements and some concern for defensive arrangements. At Wadi el Sebua a large walled village existed. At that place some hundred separate houses are grouped closely together within a semi-circular defensive wall of dry stone masonry. Complete enclosure of the village by the wall was not necessary since, as the plan shows, it was built on the edge of a cliff which drops down abruptly to the river.

The houses of this settlement are a mixture of round and roughly rectangular, but all seem to have been constructed with upright stone slabs for the

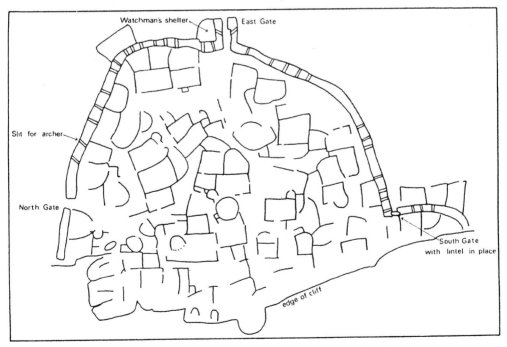

Figure 13. Fortified C-Group village at Wadi el Sebua
(*after* S. Sauneron, *Bulletin de l'Institut Français d'Archéologie Orientale*, vol. 63, 1950)

lower part, whilst the finding of considerable quantities of charred wood gives an indication of how the upper parts were built. The wall around seems certainly to have been made for defensive purposes as three gateways and thirty-two loopholes suggest. These loopholes are similar to those in Egyptian forts, to be described later, and were very probably copied from them.

The Wadi el Sebua village is so far unique for its period in Nubia, but there is another example of an even more elaborate type of settlement at Amada. This building, which has a long and varied building history, was described by its excavators, who thought it to be of the eighteenth Egyptian Dynasty, as a 'castle' and the massive nature of some of the walls makes this a not unreasonable description. Further study has shown it to be more complicated than that and to be, at least in origin, somewhat earlier. It appears to have started as a C-Group village of the normal round house type with the lower courses of the buildings of stone. Some of these round structures have been interpreted as grain silos, which some of them may have been, but the presence of hearths in others is a good indication that cooking was done

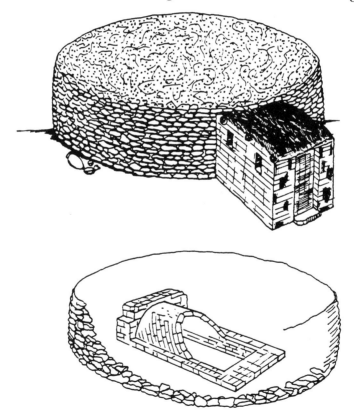

Figure 14. C-Group grave
(*after* G. Steindorff, *Aniba*, Glückstadt, 1935)

there and this implies that they were domestic dwellings. The presence of a rough dry stone wall apparently surrounding these huts suggests that this was also a defended site. Subsequently much further building took place and to the east and west of the original structure buildings of sun-dried brick were put up. The southern one has a massive, largely stone-built, wall in association with it. These buildings with rooms much larger than those previously known were for domestic purposes and by their size and impressiveness may be evidence for the existence of powerful chiefs at this period.

The most common object of C-Group manufacture is pottery – it has been found in very large numbers, mostly associated with burials (Plate 8a). Much of this pottery is similar to that of the A-Group, black topped, red burnished bowls remain common and the imported Egyptian pottery is what would be found in Egypt at the same dates. What is distinctive in C-Group pottery are the black burnished pots with incised geometric designs, often white-filled. This pottery, making its first appearance in Nubia at this time, can be considered as the characteristic pottery of the C-Group and makes possible identification of

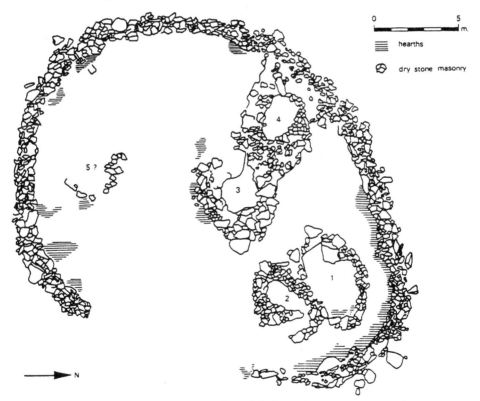

Figure 15.   Plan of C-Group house
(*after* M. Bietak and R. Engelmayer, *Osterreichische Akademie der wissenschaften, Philosophisch-Historische Klasse* 82, 1963)

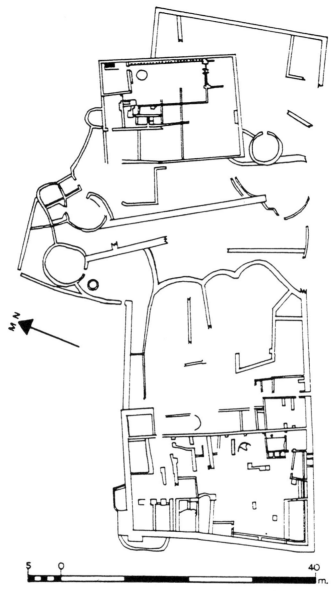

Figure 16. Plan of C-Group settlement at Amada
(*after* C. L. Woolley, *Karanog*, Philadelphia, 1911)

dwellings and burials of the period. There is considerable variety in the
incised patterns, which look as though they were originally copied from
basketry motifs. All this locally made pottery was built up by hand and the
only wheel-made pottery was that imported from Egypt.

Of other artefacts, nearly all found in graves, those of metal – mainly copper knives and mirrors – were imported from Egypt and were of well known Egyptian types. The Nubians must have made weapons and implements, and no doubt other objects, of organic materials such as wood which has perished or been eaten by termites. So we can only speculate on what they were like, though depictions of Nubian mercenaries in Egyptian service show the style of the bow which seems to have been their main weapon. The bow remained an important Nubian weapon until Christian times some 2,500 years later.

Clay figurines of women, generally steatopygous, and cattle are common and are also of types which had a long history. Of other artistic products there is no evidence. Baskets and leather objects will have been common and leather seems to have been the material used for clothing. Cloth is rare and this suggests that the Nubians had not learnt to weave – but cloth is

Figure 17. C-Group artefacts
(*after* M. Bietak and R. Engelmayer, *Osterriechische Akademie der Wissenschaften, Philosophische-Historische Klasse* 82, 1963)

subject to decay and to being eaten by termites so we may not be seeing a complete inventory of Nubian possessions. Such cloth as has been found is usually used as a wrapping for imported copper mirrors and so may itself have been imported. No traces of looms have been found at this or at other times in Nubia, but the wood of which they were made would not survive. Personal adornment consisted partly of imported Egyptian faience beads, very common in Egypt, and later made in Nubia and found at many different periods. Non-Egyptian jewellery was of such local materials as stone and shell, some of the shell coming from the Red Sea.

It has frequently been assumed that the C-Group Nubians were a pastoral cattle-herding people with large herds of cattle. This assumption is based on the large number of drawings of cattle on rocks, grave markers and other suitable surfaces as well as the clay figurines of cattle. Sometimes skulls of cattle are found associated with the graves and since much animal dung, identified as that of cattle, was mixed with the clay used for pottery this has been used as an argument to suggest that cattle were common. Certainly they seem to have been important, and perhaps prestige animals, but what we know of the Nubian environment at the time – not very different from that of today – makes it improbable that large herds could have been grazed. The small number of bones of cattle found, considerably less than those of sheep and goats, suggests that they were not a large part of Nubian subsistence. A view that cattle were socially, religiously and ceremonially important, while not kept in very large numbers, is congruent with what we know of the archaeological remains and the assumed environment of the time. Certainly from this time on cattle became a significant element in Nubian culture and they are frequently depicted in the art. The cattle tradition is well maintained by the Nilotic people of the southern Sudan today and even in Nubia, where cattle are few, feelings of prestige are associated with their ownership.

If the view of the C-Group as a pastoral people living, like some present-day pastoralists, from milk and some meat cannot be supported it must be assumed that agriculture, in this case the growing of cereal crops, was the main means of subsistence with hunting and the keeping of sheep and goats for meat as ancillary. This is the most plausible mode of subsistence. Direct evidence is lacking for grain production, although we have already seen that examples of wheat and barley are known from the A-Group and it is reasonable to suppose that these cereals were amongst the food crops grown by the C-Group. The banks of the Nile, with their annual flood, would have been suitable for the growing of these grains together with beans and dates. The recent finding of barley at Kerma (see p. 71) is additional evidence for grain growing at this time. It has been pointed out that grinding stones are not found in C-Group sites and that this is evidence that grain was not used in the diet. This is far from conclusive since in many parts of Africa grain is not ground on stones but pounded in wooden mortars which, if used by C-Group people, would not have left archaeological traces.

The period of the C-Group shows certain progress in the settlement of Nubia. Although there is no great technical advance as compared with the A-Group population, except perhaps for some more permanent building, population increased and the productive resources must have grown at the same time. Close contact with Egypt, whose trading caravans passed through the country, began to influence the life of the Nubians, though surprisingly the number of Egyptian objects in Nubian graves decreases in the later C-Group period.

It seems reasonably certain that Egyptian interest in Lower Nubia was as a route to areas which produced the luxury goods desired in Egypt. These goods – incense, ivory, ebony, leopard skins and gold – are not those likely to have been products of Nubia and they must have come from further south. If the C-Group people had developed a society with powerful chiefs, and the evidence is somewhat ambiguous, then the chiefs might have owed their position to ability to control this trade.

The Egyptian texts of the end of the Old Kingdom which give us the first information on Nubian place names certainly suggest that there were chiefs with whom the Egyptians were able to negotiate. Archaeological evidence from occupation sites of the period, except possibly for the unusual one at Amada, does not suggest any marked class stratification and if there were chiefs they cannot have lived very differently from the people they were ruling, even if they were important enough to have dealings with leaders of trading caravans and to be recognized by the Egyptians as having power to arrange treaties and co-operation.

We have already seen that Egyptian manufactured goods were being imported into Nubia during both A- and C-Group times and in 1,484 C-Group graves found in the original two surveys of Nubia over a third contained Egyptian objects. The well known pictograph, possibly of King Djer of the Egyptian first dynasty, implies that there was military as well as commercial activity and there is some evidence of an Egyptian presence during the fourth and fifth dynasties, though it appears to have been sporadic and largely confined to expeditions sent out to obtain slaves and building stone required for various prestige buildings in Egypt. Diorite, used in the temple of Khaefra (Chephren), the builder of the second pyramid at Giza, was brought from a quarry far out in the desert to the west of Toshka. At this quarry the names of several pharaohs of the fourth and fifth dynasties were found. The most southerly evidence for Old Kingdom penetration into Nubia is at Kulb in the 'Belly of the Rocks' well in the second cataract.

It does not seem that permanent Egyptian settlements were established except at Buhen, strategically placed at the downstream end of the second cataract. This town may have been founded as early as the second dynasty but certainly by the fourth dynasty a fortified town had been built there slightly to the north of the New Kingdom fort and temple. In the ruins of buildings at this place both Egyptian Old Kingdom and A-Group pottery was found together with clay seals bearing the names of fourth- and fifth-dynasty pharaohs. This shows that contact was maintained with Egypt, but there was nothing later, and subsequent Egyptian occupation was in a different location.

Emery, the excavator of Buhen, claimed that it was an important centre for copper working and as evidence for this concluded that three furnaces or kilns which he found there in an Old Kingdom context were for copper smelting. It has been suggested that the furnaces were not for copper smelting, as their internal structure with a mud brick floor half way up the interior resembles the structure of a pottery kiln rather than that of a copper smelter and the Egyptians normally smelted copper in open crucibles. There is no known source of copper in Nubia.

The first major involvement of Egypt with Nubia is seen in the sixth dynasty when a regular series of caravans began to travel from Aswan deep into Nubia. The town on the island of Elephantine at the first cataract was the most southerly town of pharaonic Egypt and remained for centuries the frontier between Egypt and Nubia. Even today, though it is several hundred kilometres north of the modern political border between Egypt and the Sudan, it remains a geographical, linguistic and ethnic frontier.

In Old Kingdom times this must have been even more clearly marked than it is now and the tombs of the local rulers in the cliff face on the west bank of the Nile across the river from the modern town of Aswan record their power and their commercial activity in Nubia and beyond.

The governors of this southern frontier of Egypt had their town on the island in the Nile still usually known by its Greek name of Elephantine, a translation of the Egyptian Abu which means elephant, presumably a reference to the ivory which passed through here on its way from south of Nubia into Egypt. Of the caravan traders of Elephantine the one who has left most information from the inscriptions in his tomb was Harkhuf who in the reign of pharaoh Mernera (c.2200 BC) made the first of four expeditions to the south to a territory which he called Yam. On this first expedition he was accompanied by his father, Iri, and the plausible suggestion has been made that Iri was already an experienced trader to the south and accompanied his son to show him the way – the inscription says that they 'explored the road to Yam' – and to introduce him to the Nubian traders. Harkhuf made three further expeditions to Yam and on his third describes how he returned with a caravan of three hundred donkeys carrying incense, ivory, ebony, leopard skins and other exotic materials. On this third expedition Harkhuf was accompanied on his return by soldiers from Yam who went with him to act as guards and perhaps to serve as mercenary soldiers in Egypt. We can see representations of similar mercenaries in some of the slightly later models of such soldiers. On his last recorded visit to Yam in the time of pharaoh Pepi II (c.2200 BC) a letter from the king, included in Harkhuf's tomb inscription, records that a dwarf had been brought back from Yam as a special present for the young king and instructions are given for the safe delivery of the dwarf to the royal court. There seems to have been excitement at court as this was the first dwarf to be brought from Yam though one had in earlier times been brought from Punt, an area almost certainly along the Red Sea coast near the present frontier of the Sudan and Ethiopia.

Harkhuf was not the only important noble from Elephantine to travel to the south but he has left the most vivid and informative account and also gives the names of a number of places in Nubia. Of these it is Yam that has been the centre of most interest since it was there that a chief was based with whom the Egyptians negotiated. There has been much discussion of the location of Yam, which certainly must have been south of the second cataract and that is beyond the area of C-Group settlement. Calculations based on the length of time that Harkhuf took to get there, some seven months from Memphis, the seat of the Egyptian royal court, has suggested to some that it should be identified with Kerma, where we now know that there was an important settlement at this time. Others have suggested that it lay much further away, and O'Connor in a recent article has argued that it was in the Shendi reach of the Nile. To account for the longer distance covered in the seven or so months would make the point of departure Elephantine rather than Memphis. These different views necessitate making a number of assumptions as to what Harkhuf's short and simple account is saying. Except for the third journey where it is explicitly said that he went by the 'oasis' road, it seems easier to interpret the text as implying travel through Nubia and to suppose that the other places through which Harkhuf travelled – Mekher, Terers and Irtjet – were in Upper and Lower Nubia, that is above and below the second cataract, and that Yam should be identified with Kerma.

Wherever Yam may have been it is certain that the traders went by land and not by the difficult river route through the cataracts. The tomb inscriptions make it quite clear that these expeditions went by land, frequently referring to 'the road' to somewhere, and they seem normally to have gone to the west before turning south and reaching the river. On their return, having once reached Egypt, presumably at Abu, they transferred to boats for the return to Memphis.

Other nobles of Aswan also visited Nubia and have left some information. Sebni records that he went to recover the body of his father who had died in the foreign land as Egyptians were always much concerned that they should be buried in their own country and that the proper burial rites be performed. Pepi-Nakht led a more aggressive expedition which went 'to hack up Wawat and Irtjet', probably both in Lower Nubia, and on a second campaign claimed to have brought the chiefs of those places to pay homage to Pepi II.

THE PAN-GRAVES

From graves, and only from graves, what appear to be a different people are seen in the late Middle Kingdom and were present during the Second Intermediate period and into the New Kingdom.

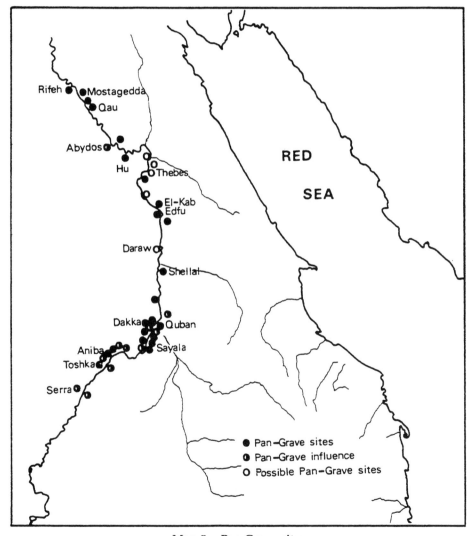

Map 5. Pan-Grave sites

Their graves, first found by Petrie at Hu in Upper Egypt and by him named 'Pan-Graves' from the shape of the burial pit, contain pottery similar to that of the C-Group, but sufficiently different not to be confused with it. The graves are not numerous but they are widespread, being found in Egypt as well as in Lower Nubia. These graves are circular pits covered with gravel mounds similar to those of the C-Group, in which sometimes leather-clad bodies were laid on their right side. Sherds of the distinctive pottery have been found as far north as Memphis in Egypt.

The graves contained not only pottery, but in the case of males, axes and daggers of Egyptian type as well as jewellery, much of it made of shell, some from the Red Sea, but also some of gold. It is usually assumed that these graves are those of mercenary soldiers in Egyptian service and they are identified, on rather shaky evidence, with the people known from Egyptian texts as the Medjay, thought to have come from the eastern desert, and to be, perhaps, ancestral to the Bega of the present day who come from the same area. The presence of Pan-Grave pottery in a number of Egyptian fortresses in Nubia, as well as in towns in Egypt strengthens the view that they were allies or mercenaries of the Egyptians.

KERMA

The most spectacular and important archaeological investigation in Nubia in recent years has been at the site of Kerma, 50 kilometres south of the third cataract, where a Swiss expedition has been working since 1977 and uncovering the remains of a town which dates back to about 2,400 BC. This town and the religious buildings associated with it show that there was a much earlier development of urban civilization than had been thought possible in Nubia or elsewhere in Africa so far south. The size of the site, located in an area with a rich agricultural potential, suggests that it was a centre of a powerful indigenous state which traded with Egypt and controlled the flow of luxury articles which the Egyptians desired.

The site, made obvious by the two enormous mud-brick structures, known locally as the Western and Eastern Deffufa (Plates 10a, 10b), from a Nubian word used for brick ruins, had originally been excavated and studied by an American expedition directed by Reisner in 1913–16. This work examined not only the deffufas but also a group of buildings close to the western one and a large number of cemeteries ranging in date from early Kerma times to Meroitic.

There has been much speculation about the date of the site and the purpose of the unique building, the Western Deffufa. The large number of Egyptian and Egyptianizing objects found led Reisner to suggest that there had been an Egyptian occupation and that this complex had been the fortified palace of the governor. From the presence of broken alabaster vases with the names of Pepi I and Pepi II he assumed that there had been occupation from as early as the end of the Old Kingdom, but since they were found in association with Middle Kingdom fragments and a large number (565) of mud seals from various containers, also of Middle Kingdom date, the logical principle that the latest object in a deposit is a *terminus post quem* makes it far more likely that they represent the results of trading activity in the Middle Kingdom, though it is possible that the alabaster pieces were survivals from objects brought by the Egyptian traders of the Old Kingdom.

The recent work has shown that the Western Deffufa was originally built as a religious structure, somewhat like an Egyptian temple of the period, but was modified and changed many times and its architectural evolution over a long period, in the words of the excavator, 'témoigne de l'attachement des habitants à leurs croyances'. He goes on to say that the changes and re-modelling from the end of Middle Kerma times (c.2000 BC) give 'l'impression que ce quartier de la cité est constamment en chantier'. At least twelve different building stages can be identified.

The town which stood close to the Western Deffufa started as quite a small one with round huts of light materials and a defensive wall. These were destroyed to allow enlargement but it may well have been here that lay the capital of Yam in the time of Harkhuf. By the Middle Kingdom the town was much enlarged. Powerful fortifications were built, as well as the Western Deffufa, and in addition to rectangular mud-brick houses with several rooms each, a circular hut, some 15 to 16 metres in diameter was erected, perhaps as an audience hall or for other ceremonial purposes. There was also industrial activity and a workshop and a furnace for the smelting of copper was identified, though the source of copper ore remains a mystery.

The cemeteries already partly investigated by Reisner include a number of large mounds containing multiple burials and the large brick construction of the Eastern Deffufa, somewhat smaller and less complex than the western one. It consisted of two long rooms each with four columns in a line along the centre of the room. Only the stone bases of these columns remain and the columns themselves, presumably, though not certainly, of stone, would have supported wooden beams as part of the roof construction. The walls of the deffufa are of mud brick and of massive construction, being about 10 metres thick and similar to the brick work of the Western Deffufa. It is confidently supposed that this building, standing as it does close to the cemetery, and another similar but much more destroyed one, were funerary chapels associated with the large mound graves close by.

These mound graves, of which eight were found to the south of the cemetery, are the largest burial structures known from Nubia. The largest of them, known as K III, 90 metres in diameter, contained, as did some others, a main

Figure 18. Reconstruction of audience hall at Kerma
(*from* Professor C. Bonnet)

central corridor with mud-brick walls running at right angles, either to provide a rigid structure for the sand and gravel mound erected over it or to act
as rooms to contain funeral offerings or the bodies of sacrificed royal com-
panions or slaves found in large numbers; in the case of K X, 322 human
skeletons were found.

In K III a statue of the Egyptian lady Sennuwy (Plate 13) was found in the central corridor and elsewhere in the mound fragments of a statue of her husband, Hepjefa. Hepjefa is known to have been a noble of Asyut in Egypt in the time of Sesostris I (1971–1928 BC) and his tomb is at that place. The finding of these statues caused Reisner to conclude that Hepjefa had been a governor of the region for the Egyptian pharaoh, had died at Kerma and been buried in K II with local rites. Apart from the improbability that an Egyptian, who valued the performance of the proper traditional Egyptian funeral rites very highly (as evidenced by Sebni's expedition into Nubia to recover his father's body) would be buried with foreign rites, the dating of the tomb to the time of Sesostris I is now shown to be wrong, since an object with the name of Amenemmes III, who lived about 130 years later, was found, as well as scarabs and an ivory piece of the First Intermediate period.

The current view of the chronology of the large mound graves is that, contrary to the view of Reisner who supposed them to be of the Middle Kingdom, they date from rather late in the Second Intermediate period and are approximately contemporary with Hyksos rule in Egypt. This causes a re-assessment of the Egyptian presence at Kerma where Reisner had assumed a considerable number of Egyptians to be present as administrators, soldiers and artisans in what was claimed to have been an Egyptian colonial occupation.

The presence of Egyptian statues needs to be explained, and there are a number of other fragments in addition to the statues of Hepjefa and his wife. The presence of an Egyptian Middle Kingdom fortified frontier at the second cataract, to be described below, makes it far more likely that Kerma was the centre of an independent Nubian state – probably Yam, and which would become Kush. The main manifestations there are certainly indigenous, and it can be suggested that Egyptian objects are present as a result of trade or as gifts.

Further work on the cemeteries in recent years has thrown more light on Kerma burial customs and has provided evidence for social stratification in Kerma society. The burials were very rich in grave goods and have provided much new information about the culture of Kerma. A study of the bodies has shown that the Kerma people generally resembled modern Nubians and are not substantially different from the other dwellers in Nubia in A- and C-Group times – though, as in the modern population, there was considerable variability. This information strengthens the argument for continuity in Nubian history compared with the invasion and immigration interpretations for cultural change that used to be popular.

Details of clothing are known – loin cloths of leather were worn and bodies were frequently wrapped in leather or linen sometimes decorated with ostrich egg-shell or faience beads. Leather sandals were worn and women had leather hair nets. Burials were accompanied by bronze mirrors, ostrich feather fans, and jewellery of wood, faience, semi-precious stones, ivory and bone as well as leather bags, the leather being made from goat and sheep skins as well as from cattle (Plate 11b). Some men were buried with their bows and laid on an oxhide. Sheep and dogs were put in the graves and in some the sheep had an elaborate head-dress of ostrich feathers fastened by leather thongs. The strewing of barley and flax on the sacrificed sheep shows not only an interesting aspect of the burial customs but gives concrete evidence for the growing of these crops. The placing of ox skulls around the edge of some of the larger burial mounds, not only at Kerma but also in other places, such as the large cemetery at Sai island, shows that there was an important cattle cult and that there were large numbers of the animals. Kerma, with its wide agricultural lands, was one of the few areas in Nubia that could support herds of cattle.

Of the artefacts made by the Kerma people the most distinctive and easily recognized are the pots (Plate 11a). Perhaps following on from a tradition going back to the A-Group the Kerma people developed the manufacture of

Figure 19. Reconstruction of sacrificial ram's head-dress
(*from* Professor C. Bonnet)

71

polished red and black-topped pottery to a degree of refinement never previously seen. These pots were so finely and delicately made that for a long time it was thought that they were made on a potter's wheel. Further examination has shown that this was not so, and they were built up by hand as was all indigenous Nubian pottery up to this time. The only wheel-made ceramics were imported from Egypt.

It is this distinctive pottery, found at many Kerma-period sites in Nubia, as far upstream as the fourth cataract and even as far away from the river as the Gash river in the east, that has made it possible to establish a chronological system for Kerma material and, though Kerma itself was the main urban centre, many other sites are known, of which the most extensive is the large cemetery of mound graves on the island of Sai. The detailed study of Kerma sites and material made by Brigitte Gratien was completed before much of the new information from Kerma itself had been obtained but the main categorization into 'Kerma ancien' starting in c.2400 BC, 'Kerma moyen' c.2000 BC to the time of the Egyptian thirteenth dynasty, 'Kerma classique', flourishing in the Second Intermediate period (c. 1786–1567 BC), and 'Kerma récent', equivalent to the Egyptian eighteenth dynasty, still stands. It appears from the chronology established by Gratien that the high point of Kerma culture was during the Second Intermediate period when it spread north of the second cataract and is found throughout Lower Nubia. One grave containing Kerma pottery has even been found as far north as Abydos in Egypt. The Kerma culture appears at about the same time as that of the C-Group and there are many resemblances – so many that some have supposed the two to be, at least in origin, the same culture and the same people. This may be and the chronological overlap certainly seems correct, but the material remains, though in some cases showing similarities, have sufficient difference to suggest that there were two distinct groups living in Nubia at the time.

THE EGYPTIAN PRESENCE IN NUBIA

Although there is little to suggest that Egypt had a permanent presence in Nubia during the Old Kingdom except at Buhen, by the Middle Kingdom (c.2000 BC) the situation had changed radically and although there is no evidence for occupation during the eleventh dynasty, by the time of Amenemmes I (c. 2000–1970 BC) there were military expeditions 'to overthrow' Wawat in Lower Nubia. His successor, Sesostris I, established and garrisoned several forts in Lower Nubia, at Ikkur, Quban and Aniba. These forts, with their thick mud brick walls and round bastions, were the first of this type to be built and served as models for later ones. An inscription from Buhen, where there had been a fort since Old Kingdom times, shows a line of Nubian prisoners being presented to Sesostris by the god Montu and describes military campaigns. Subsequently a large number of forts were built in the time of Sesostris III at what was the southern frontier of Egyptian-occupied Nubia. These massive forts, built of mud brick with timber reinforcements, were strategically placed at Semna, south of the second cataract where a line of hard rock narrows the river to only some 30 metres wide at low river (Plate 14a). The forts, on either side of the river, of Semna and Kumma (now vanished under the waters of Lake Nubia), were supported by another on an island in the river at Uronarti (Plate 14b). South of Semna the fort of Semna south, originally on the river bank, was of rather modest size with a 9 metre wide main wall enclosing a square with a side of 52 metres. This small fort can be presumed to have been a police post for controlling travellers and traders coming from the south. A wall ran from Semna south along the river. It seems that it was to protect land traffic to Mirgissa further north on the west bank.

These forts were different from the rectangular ones of the flat river banks of Lower Nubia and were cleverly laid out to take advantage of the local topography, being built on rocky promontories and adapting their defences to these irregular shapes. Although Semna was the main frontier defence other forts were established downstream, Shelfak, Askut, Dabenarti, Mirgissa, Kor and Buhen. Some of these were on islands and the group shows a very well planned system of defence in depth for this important southern frontier. It could be noted, before these forts were inundated by Lake Nubia, that it would have been possible to communicate from one to the other by visual signals, smoke or heliograph, along the whole line of river at least from Semna to Mirgissa.

A group of documents, the Semna despatches, of the reign of Amenemmes III gives interesting information about the activities of the garrisons of the forts and demonstrates that they were not just static garrisons but carried out patrols, often using Medjay for this purpose, to keep an eye on wandering natives. They also show that there was a bureaucratic organization for sending reports back to Egypt and for communicating between the forts. This careful strategic placing, with two further forts to the north of Shelfak on the west bank and Askut on an island before the second cataract is reached, suggests that the forts were established both to defend the outermost frontier of Egypt and to control commercial traffic along the Nile. Sesostris III erected two large stelae with virtually identical inscriptions, one at Semna and on the island of Uronarti in his sixteenth year. The text of the one at Semna says:

> I have made my boundary further south than my fathers, I have added to what was bequeathed me. I am a king who speaks and acts, what my heart plans is done by my arm. One who attacks to conquer, who is swift to succeed, in whose heart a plan does not slumber. Considerate

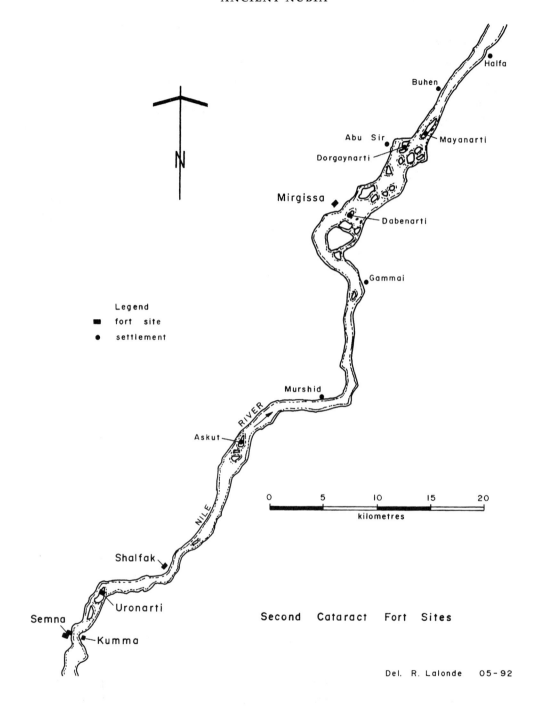

N

Legend
■ fort site
● settlement

Halfa

Buhen

Abu Sir
Dorgaynarti
Mayanarti

Mirgissa

Dabenarti

Gammai

Murshid

NILE RIVER

Askut

0   5   10   15   20
kilometres

Shalfak

Uronarti

Semna

Kumma

Second Cataract Fort Sites

Del. R. Lalonde 05-92

Map 6. Egyptian forts at the second cataract

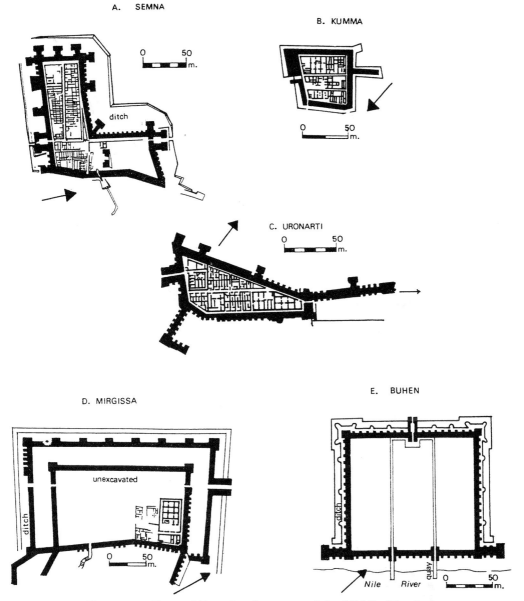

Figure 20. Plans of Egyptian fortresses of the Middle Kingdom
(*after* W. B. Emery, *Egypt in Nubia*, London, 1965)

to clients, steady in mercy, merciless to the foe who attacks him. One
who attacks him who would attack. Who stops when one stops, who
replies to a matter as befits it. To stop when attacked is to make bold
the foe's heart, attack is valor, retreat is cowardice, a coward is he who
is driven from his border.

75

Since the Nubian listens to the word of mouth, to answer him is to make him retreat.

Attack him, he will turn his back, retreat, he will start attacking. They are not people one respects, they are wretches, craven-hearted. My majesty has seen it, it is not an untruth. I have captured their women, I have carried off their dependents, gone to their wells, killed their cattle, cut down their grain, set fire to it.

As my father lives for me, I speak the truth! It is no boast that comes from my mouth. As for any son of mine who shall maintain this border which my majesty had made, he is my son, born to my majesty. The true son is he who champions his father, who guards the border of his begetter. But he who abandons it, who fails to fight for it, he is not my son, he was not born to me.

Now my majesty has had an image made of my majesty, at this border which my majesty has made, in order that you maintain it, in order that you fight for it.

(Translation from M. Lichtheim, *Ancient Egyptian Literature*, I, 119–20.)

It should be noted that the term Nubians in this text is used as a convenient translation of *nehesi*, the word used by the Egyptians for the inhabitants of the region. It does not necessarily imply that these people were ethnically or linguistically the same as modern Nubians.

An earlier inscription of the eighth year of Sesostris is more specific in its control of local travellers and merchants and says:

Southern boundary, made in the year 8, under the majesty of the King of Upper and Lower Egypt, Khakaura Sesostris III who is given life forever and ever; in order to prevent any Nubian from crossing it, by water or by land, with a ship, or any herds of the herds of the Nubians; except a Nubian who shall come to do trading in Iken, or with a commission. Every good thing shall be done with them, but without allowing a ship of the Nubians to pass by Heh, going downstream forever.

(Translation from Emery, *Egypt in Nubia*, 157.)

(In the original translation the word Negro is used where I have put Nubian.)

Sesostris certainly refers to Semna and the most probable identification of Iken is with Mirgissa. This inscription, together with the two of year 16, make it quite clear that the intention was to have a frontier at Semna, an obvious place, and only to permit those with business at Iken, or a permit, to pass, and there is no information to suggest that the Egyptians of the Middle Kingdom went further south.

Mirgissa, identified as the ancient Iken, is on the west bank overlooking the second cataract and is the largest of the forts. In addition to its strong fortifications, appropriate to its strategic position, it provided evidence of the supply, storage and manufacture of weapons. Stone arrow and spear heads were found as well as specially shaped stones on which the leather to make shields was stretched and the wooden handles for the shields. A mud slipway along which boats were pulled to get them past an extreme point in the cataract was found – the prints of the feet of those who pulled the boats as well as the marks of the boats' keels were all clearly marked in the sun-dried mud. There were also domestic houses and a riverside port and Mirgissa seems to have been the main centre for handling trade with the south.

North of the second cataract the forts take on a different aspect. They are no longer sited on hill tops or islands difficult of access but, as the topography of Lower Nubia demands, were on the flat land along the river and, no longer needing to conform to the contours of hills, were more regular in their shape and lay-out.

Their function was somewhat different from those of the frontier and though there was no frontier to be defined and defended against the people of Kerma or the C-Group they were still strongly fortified. Some of them, notably those at Aniba and Ikkur, are close to important areas of C-Group settlement and were perhaps placed there to ensure peaceful passage of trading vessels along the navigable stretch of river between the first and second cataracts. It is noticeable that they are strongly defended on the side away from the river and it may be that in some part they were to hold off attacks from desert-dwelling peoples.

The frontier forts were abandoned in the thirteenth dynasty after about 1720 BC and there has been discussion as to whether they were attacked, and perhaps captured, by the C-Group Nubians. There are signs of burning in several of the forts which may have been done during or after attacks, though it has also been argued that the forts were too strong to be captured unless the garrisons had been withdrawn and this therefore suggests that the burning was done deliberately by the retreating Egyptians so as to deny use of the forts to the Nubians.

Whatever the reason – collapse of central power in Egypt or the deliberate withdrawal of troops to oppose the Hyksos invaders of Egypt from Asia – Egyptian occupation of the area of the second cataract came to an end and even some forts downstream of the second cataract, notably Buhen, show signs of abandonment.

CHAPTER 5

EGYPTIAN OCCUPATION IN THE NEW KINGDOM

◆

Whatever the reasons for the Egyptian withdrawal from Nubia at the end of the Middle Kingdom – and these may have been due to increased disorder in Egypt as a result of the fragmentation of the country after dynasty 12, or to the need for troops to attempt to repel the Hyksos – there seems little doubt but that it was the unification and militarization of Egypt necessary for the expulsion of the Hyksos, under the leadership of a family from Thebes in Upper Egypt, that was responsible for a new and successful attempt to occupy Nubia. After the withdrawal of Egyptian garrisons from the forts built in the Middle Kingdom there was a period of independent C-Group and Kerma life and some of the forts were occupied by local people. This is especially clear at Mirgissa where such people occupied part of the fort and established a cemetery.

Not only had the ruler of Kush (very likely Kerma) shown himself hostile and been asked by the Hyksos king to join him in crushing Egypt, but the riches of the south, already well known from the trading activities of the Old and Middle Kingdoms, beckoned. This time Egypt was not content with a fortified frontier which could control trade, which was largely in the hands of native peoples, but was determined to take full control by occupying Nubia as far as the fourth cataract and to penetrate even further.

This was occupation in a colonial style, and Egyptian military and civil administrators ruled in the former territory of Kerma and built towns and temples and imposed Egyptian rule so effectively that it lasted for nearly five hundred years and left a permanent impression on the native inhabitants. This occupation was not carried out overnight and much hard fighting was necessary before Egyptian control was fully established. Sporadic rebellions called for campaigns by many of the Pharaohs.

The revival of Egyptian military strength is shown in the account given by

Kamose, who describes military campaigns to drive the Hyksos out of Egypt, and in an important document, the Kamose stela, recounts the capture of a letter from the Hyksos king Auserra to a king of Kush in which it is suggested that they form an alliance to divide Egyptian territory between them. In the translation of Labib Habachi the text reads,

> I captured his message beyond the oasis going southward to Kush in a written letter. I found on it the following in writing by the hand: Auserre, son of Re Apophis greets my son, the ruler of Kush. Why have you risen as a ruler without letting me know? Have you seen what Egypt has done against me? The ruler who is in it, Kamose, is attacking me on my soil, but I am not attacking him in the way he had done against you. He chose the two lands to persecute them, my land and yours, and he has ravaged them. Come, navigate downstream, do not be afraid. Behold he is here with me; there is no one who will be waiting for you in this Egypt, for I will not let him go until you have arrived. Then we shall divide the towns of this Egypt.

It seems that Kushite support for the Hyksos was not effective, and a graffito at Armenna in Lower Nubia gives Kamose's name and implies that he had occupied, or at least campaigned in, that area, though this should not be taken to mean that there was full Egyptian occupation. It seems that Kamose took the opportunity of a new ruler in Kush, implied in the captured letter, to ensure the safety of the southern frontier before attacking the Hyksos in northern Egypt.

The occupation of Nubia began effectively with Ahmose, Kamose's brother and first king of the eighteenth Egyptian dynasty, an account of whose campaign is given in the tomb inscription of Ahmose son of Ebana at El Kab who says,

> Now when his majesty (King Ahmose) had slain the nomads of Asia, he sailed south to Khent-hen-nefer, to destroy the Nubian Bowmen. His majesty made a great slaughter among them, and I brought spoil from there: two living men and three hands. Then I was rewarded with gold once again, and two female slaves were given to me. His majesty journeyed north, his heart rejoicing in valor and victory. He had conquered Southerners, Northerners.
>
> Then I conveyed King Djeserkare (Amenhotep I), the justified, when he sailed south to Kush, to enlarge the borders of Egypt. His majesty smote that Nubian Bowman in the midst of his army. They were carried off in fetters, none missing, the fleeing destroyed as if they had never been. Now I was in the van of our troops and I fought really well. His majesty saw my valor. I carried off two hands and presented them to his majesty. Then his people and his cattle were pursued, and I carried

79

off a living captive and presented him to his majesty. I brought his majesty back to Egypt in two days from 'Upper Well', and was rewarded with gold. I brought back two female slaves as booty, apart from those that I had presented to his majesty. Then they made me a Warrior of the Ruler'.

(Translation from M. Lichtheim, *Ancient Egyptian Literature*, II, 13–14.)

A temple with a door jamb bearing the name of Pharaoh Ahmose was built at Buhen and it is likely that he either repaired the original Middle Kingdom fort or built a new one at this strategic point immediately down stream of the second cataract. The name of this Pharaoh also occurs at Sai island but it is not certain that this is evidence for his presence so far south and the inscription may post-date him.

Under the next Pharaoh, Amenophis I, who reigned from 1545 BC, penetration went as far as Semna and Uronarti since his name has been found associated with Thuwra the viceroy of Nubia in years 7 and 8 of the Pharaoh. Ahmose son of Ebana was still active in this reign and his inscription tells of the capture of a local chief. This suggests aggressive Egyptian action from very early in the New Kingdom and, although there may be some hyperbole in the Egyptian accounts, Nubian resistance seems to have been slight.

The next advance was in the reign of Tuthmosis I when the decisive occupation of the whole stretch of land along the river to beyond the fourth

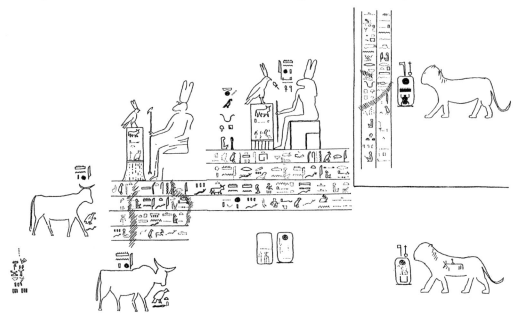

Figure 21. Kurgus boundary inscription
(*after* A. J. Arkell, *A History of the Sudan to 1821*, London, 1961)

cataract was made. A fort is said to have been established at Tumbus (Plate 15) by the third cataract, and further upstream beyond the difficult country of the fourth cataract an inscription was carved on a prominent rock at Kurgus beside a small mud-brick fort. This is the furthest up-stream evidence for Egyptian occupation and no objects or inscriptions have been found south of this place, though there is no inherent impossibility in further Egyptian penetration along the comparatively easy stretch of river to the junction of the river Atbara with the Nile.

The campaign of Tuthmosis I may have put an end to the Kerma state, though archaeological evidence from Kerma has not confirmed this. It has been suggested that at least the Western Deffufa was attacked and burned. The vivid account by Ahmose son of Ebana of the journey back to Egypt with many prisoners and with the body of a local ruler – perhaps that of Kerma – hanging head down from the prow of the ship shows that a major victory had been gained. Ahmose's words are:

> Then his majesty (was informed that the Nubian). ... At this his majesty became enraged like a leopard. His majesty shot, and his first arrow pierced the chest of that foe. Then those (enemies turned to flee), helpless before his Uraeus. A slaughter was made among them; their dependents were carried off as living captives. His majesty journeyed north, all foreign lands in his grasp, and that wretched Nubian Bowman head downward at the bow of his majesty's ship Falcon.
> (Translation from M. Lichtheim, *Ancient Egyptian Literature*, II, 14.)

The death of Tuthmosis I, in 1505 BC, and his succession by Tuthmosis II was followed, probably not coincidentally, by a Nubian revolt in the region of Kush, that is south of the second cataract. This revolt, though having some initial success, was firmly put down with much slaughter and a son of the ruler of 'miserable Kush', the usual epithet used by the Egyptians, was taken back to Egypt. From this time on Nubia seems to have been mainly peaceful, though Tuthmosis III claimed military victory and slaughter of Nubians in an inscription in the temple of Karnak. The strong tendency to exaggeration and self-glorification by the Pharaohs makes it difficult to accept many such claims with confidence unless the victory inscriptions are found in the territory where the victory is claimed. A number of expeditions by pharaohs or by military commanders acting in their name are recorded throughout the New Kingdom. It seems likely that these were not against the inhabitants of the Nile valley, who were becoming increasingly Egyptianized, but punitive campaigns against dwellers in the desert margins who were a continual threat to the settled agricultural peoples of the river banks.

Egyptian control over Nubia was highly organized and Egyptian culture widespread, and though it may not have effected the majority of the native inhabitants – descendants of the C-Group and Kerma people, maintaining much the same style of life and achievement – there is evidence for an acculturation by local chiefs who began to adopt Egyptian styles and customs.

Egypt established a colonial administration quite unlike the system that they used in Western Asia where the rulers of city states were maintained in power by the Egyptians and controlled by treaty relations. In Nubia a form of direct rule was established under an Egyptian governor or viceroy. The official who was appointed as governor bore the title of 'King's son and overseer of foreign countries'. The first one of whom we know was Thuwra who was appointed in the time of Pharaoh Amenophis I, being first known to us as commandant of the fort at Buhen where he was perhaps responsible for its refurbishment. Somewhat later, in the time of Tuthmosis IV the title was changed to that of 'King's Son of Kush' but in neither case was the title more than an honorary one and these high civil servants seem not to have been relatives of the Pharaoh.

The power of these governors, or viceroys as they are usually called, was very great and it was not long before the southern part of Upper Egypt, up stream from El Kab, was also placed under their control. There were two deputy governors, one controlling Wawat, the northern part of Nubia up to the second cataract, with his residence at Aniba, and the other based at Amara West, at least during the nineteenth dynasty, to administer Kush. Military commanders and a whole host of other officials are also known. Egyptian garrisons and Egyptian officials exercised power and were much concerned with the collection of taxes which, at least on occasion, were taken to the Pharaoh in person by the governor. These taxes consisted of the many precious and exotic products of Africa – gold, ivory, ebony, ostrich feathers and eggs, wild animals, incense and various precious and semi-precious stones. Known in moderation from Old Kingdom times, these products now came to Egypt in far greater quantity and there are many depictions in New Kingdom tombs of African people bringing such goods. The increase in wealth from the occupation of Nubia had a profound effect in Egypt and increased greatly the wealth of pharaohs, the priesthood and the aristocracy. It was primarily gold which made for this rapidly expanding wealth. Its use became widespread in Egypt, and the whole of the ancient Near East came to learn of the vast wealth held by the pharaohs. When the rulers of small city states of Palestine and Syria wrote to the Pharaoh requesting presents of gold they were not far wrong when they claimed that gold was everywhere in the Pharaoh's domain.

There was also a steady supply of human beings. The role of slavery in ancient Egypt is not well understood but there are enough references in the texts to prisoners and depictions of them in tomb paintings and sculptured reliefs and on memorial buildings to make it clear that considerable numbers were taken to Egypt.

Many of these prisoners are shown as negroes and it is only from this period that negroes are shown in Egyptian art. It seems from study of skeletal remains that the population of Lower Nubia was not, in the main, negro and it was only after Egyptian penetration south of the second cataract that depictions of distinctively negro people become common in Egyptian art. From this time on they increase considerably, negroes often being shown as prisoners or as bringers of tribute or taxes, as in the tomb of Rekhmire. The Egyptians certainly came to regard such people as the normal inhabitants of the south and depictions of negroes become the stereotype of southerners in the frequent representations of the southern and northern enemies of Egypt as in the well known box of Tutankhamen or beneath the seated statues of Ramesses II at Abu Simbel. It seems likely that much of the work of restoring forts and erection of new buildings as well as the uncongenial work of quarrying for stone was done by these prisoners.

As a consequence of the invasion, occupation and settlement of Nubia many Egyptian buildings were established and towns, forts and temples are to be found in many places. The development of Egyptian occupation and the building activities that went with it can be seen to have gone through several stages. In the first place there was re-occupation and restoration at places of Middle Kingdom activity. These included forts and towns at such sites as Kubban which guards the entrance to the Wadi Allaqi with its important gold mines where there is an inscription recording the accession as Pharaoh of Tuthmosis I; Ikkur on the other side of the river; Aniba, to become an important administrative centre, and Buhen. In addition to the forts and temples built within them, other temples were built in open areas. Of these temples in Lower Nubia one at Amada was built in the reign of Amenophis II, one at Wadi el Sebua by Amenophis III, and several small ones during the period from Tuthmosis I to Tuthmosis III. Buhen was of special importance and is the most fully excavated and studied. Originally excavated in 1909–10 by MacIver and Woolley, it was further examined by Emery in the 1960s and he described the alterations and strengthening of the original Middle Kingdom structure in the following words:

> The old fortress walls were rebuilt and strengthened, the lower ramparts and ditch being filled and covered by a brick paved road which surrounded the whole structure, making it a citadel in the centre of the new fortifications, which were built on a much larger and more elaborate scale. A ditch, 6 metres wide and 2 metres deep, was dug, forming a perimeter of about one mile, and behind this were built the

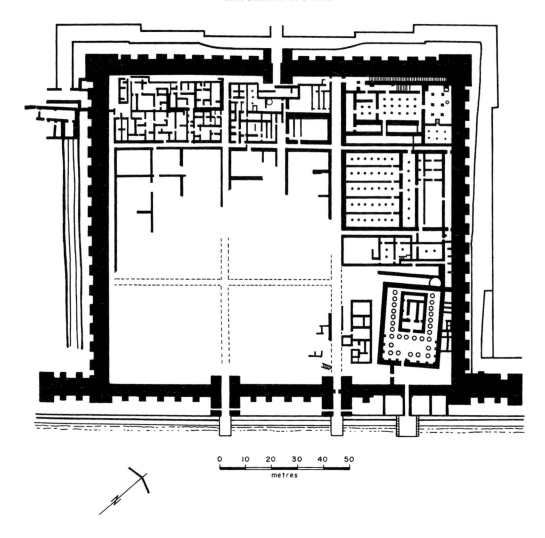

Figure 22. Plan of Buhen fortress
(*after* W. B. Emery, *Egypt in Nubia*, London, 1965)

walls which enclosed the new town. These were of great strength: 5 metres thick, at least 12 metres high, with rectangular towers set at intervals on the exterior face. The plan of these fortifications, unlike that of the Middle Kingdom structure, was irregular in shape with wide salients, the largest of which was situated approximately in the centre, on the western side facing the desert. Within this salient was a great gatehouse with a rock-cut causeway which crossed the ditch and was the principal entrance to the fortress.

Within the fortress there was a temple dedicated to Horus of Buhen built in the time of Queen Hatshepsut over the remains of an earlier one dating from the Middle Kingdom. There are examples of Hatshepsut's name having been cut out and replaced by that of her successor Tuthmosis III. The painted reliefs of this temple are of very high quality and show royalty making offerings to Horus and to other gods. The temple has now been removed and re-erected in the grounds of the museum in Khartoum (Plates 20a, 20b).

South of the second cataract, the old forts of the original Middle Kingdom frontier were scarcely touched and there is little evidence even for re-occupation, though small temples were built at Semna, Kumma and Uronarti where Sesostris III, the establisher of the frontier in the twelfth dynasty, was worshipped as a god and the small numbers of priests, who were required for the temple service, lived.

The main effort in this southern region of Kush dating from the late eighteenth and nineteenth dynasties was the establishment of new walled towns to house military garrisons, civil administrators and the priests needed to service the temples which were included in them. These towns, mostly on the west bank of the river, are, in geographical order Amara West, Sai, Sadenga, Soleb and Sesebi, though it is not clear that there were major urban centres at all these places. Where there has been sufficient excavation to show the main elements of the towns they are seen to have been more or less rectangular enclosures with rather light mud-brick walls with square towers placed along them. Kemp has pointed out that these walls resemble very closely those that surrounded the temples in Egypt as a *temenos* to demarcate the sacred area rather than as town defences and suggests that in essence that is what they were, though used in Nubia rather differently since in a number of cases they surrounded domestic occupation as well as temples.

Amara West, though still not fully published forty years after the close of the excavations, is a good example of this new type of colonial settlement and the general lay-out, perhaps originally planned to be a regular grid, can be seen in places though often overlaid by later buildings which do not adhere strictly to the earlier plan and give rise to a number of narrow streets. It contains a temple, built in the reign of Ramesses II, and an elaborate complex of buildings which included the residence of the deputy governor of Kush. Although Amara West has the usual enclosure wall, defence against an enemy does not seem to have been a primary consideration and there was occupation outside the wall with, in one case, a house built up against it and using the town fortification as a back wall. There was also a small building which appears to have been a shrine to a snake cult (Plates 21a, 21b).

Further south on the large island of Sai was another walled town probably founded in the time of Amenophis II, or even earlier, and therefore built before other settlements in the region. Major excavations have been carried out here by a French expedition, led by Professor Vercoutter, from 1954 to 1957 and from 1969 to 1981, and many traces of the New Kingdom occupation from the eighteenth to the twentieth dynasties were found, though much overlaid by later building activities some as late as the Turkish times of the sixteenth and seventeenth centuries. Statues and inscriptions of several kings of the eighteenth dynasty from as early as Amenophis I were found, as well as remains of at least two temples, and there was also a large Egyptian cemetery. Egyptian occupation did not lead to elimination of the native inhabitants and the island is very rich in burials of the Kerma people (Plate 17a).

Soleb and Sadenga, close together on the west bank a little way south of Sai, have temples built by, or at least in the time of, Amenophis III and dedicated to the worship of that Pharaoh and his Queen, Tiye. The Sadenga temple is much destroyed and little remains but that at Soleb, built on a large scale, has been carefully studied and partly restored in a series of campaigns from 1957 to 1964. It is the largest and finest pharaonic temple in Nubia and its existence is good evidence for the peaceful control which Egypt exercised in the region in the latter part of the eighteenth dynasty.

It can be presumed that there was a town associated with these temples, but no trace of it has been found. The Soleb temple was enclosed by a wall, but this seems more like the usual wall around an Egyptian temple than a town defence and no evidence for domestic occupation has been found within the area enclosed. This temple, somewhat similar to the temple at Luxor in Egypt, of the same date, deserves some detailed description. The lay-out is the standard one for Egyptian temples with an entrance flanked by towers, known to Egyptologists as pylons, leading into an outer court with a colonnade round the four sides, this court being the only part of the temple into which the populace could enter, the remainder of the building being reserved for the priesthood. Beyond this is an inner court of similar style which leads to the hypostyle hall, a hall with many columns, and then to the sanctuary. The walls and the columns are covered with relief sculpture giving the name of the Pharaoh, showing the usual scenes of the making of offerings to the god, and also lists of captured towns of both Nubia and Western Asia. The whole purpose of the temple is to show the power and might of the Pharaoh and to emphasize that Egypt ruled widely over the ancient world. Some 800 metres to the west of the temple was a New Kingdom cemetery consisting of forty-seven tombs nearly all being multi-burials. From the traces of superstructure it appears that many of them were surmounted by small pyramids of a type familiar from tombs at Deir-el-Medina in Egypt.

Going south again Sesebi is reached where a ditched enclosure, presumably of the early eighteenth dynasty was overlaid by a much larger (270 by 200 metres) town built at the time of Akhenaten when three temples, including a shrine to the Aten, were erected and storage and residential areas were included. Little detail was obtained from excavations due to the considerable erosion at the site.

The earlier site of Kerma shows no sign of New Kingdom activity and in the now rich agricultural areas of the Dongola stretch of the river, which were probably similarly prosperous in earlier times, there is little to show the Egyptian presence. This may be illusory since greater population in this area at nearly all times will have caused greater destruction of early monuments. New Kingdom blocks have been found at Tabo, on Argo island, where much later a Meroitic temple was built, possibly on a site used in pharaonic times.

At Kawa, on the east bank opposite the modern town of Dongola, are the still unexcavated remains of what is almost certainly a large New Kingdom town. This site is thought to be identified with Gem Aten, founded by Akhenaten, but the earliest dated building so far known is a small temple of the time of Tutankhamen in which Ramesses II also carved his name. The town remained important for a long time and subsequent buildings of Napatan and Meroitic times will be described later.

Between Kawa and the important sites near to Gebel Barkal and the fourth cataract no New Kingdom sites are known. This may be due to lack of archaeological survey in the area, and the great quantities of sand that have accumulated on both banks of the river may be concealing evidence of occupation of this period. The other possibility is that the Egyptians, like others since, by-passed the big bend in the river and took the short cut by land, now known as the Sikkat el-Miheila, which from near to Kawa cuts across the desert in a south-eastern direction to reach the river again not far from Gebel Barkal. However this may be, it is not until Barkal is reached that New Kingdom occupation is once more found. At this place there is a dramatic addition to the landscape. Out of a flat plain which stretches away on both sides of the river there rises a hill known as Barkal, or Gebel Barkal with *gebel* meaning a hill or mountain in Arabic. This hill stands about 2 kilometres from the river on the right side of the river and forms a most noticeable and famous landmark. This would seem to be an obvious place for the Egyptians to have placed a garrison and built a temple. It is, except for the small advance post at Kurgus, the up-river terminus of their expeditions and of the stretch of riverain Nubia that they conquered. Below the mountain they built a temple. Perhaps the first was from the time of Tuthmosis III since his name has been found there, as also has that of Tuthmosis IV. It seems, however, that the large temple to the god Amun which was rebuilt and added to in later times was the work of Horemheb or perhaps Seti I although, as seems inevitable, Ramesses II was also active here. Ramesses was certainly the builder of the southern chapel.

In Napatan times the area became the centre of an independent state, as will be described in the next chapter, but even under the Egyptians it must

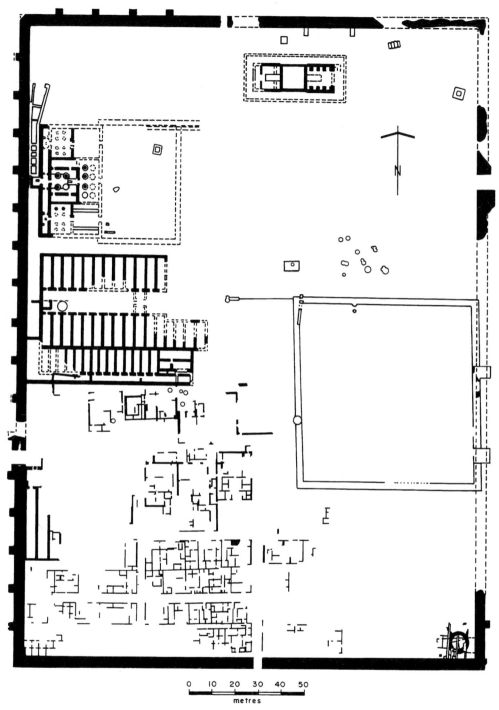

0 10 20 30 40 50
metres

Figure 23.   Plan of Sesebi town
(*after* H. W. Fairman, *Journal of Egyptian Archaeology* 24, 1938)

have been of importance. It is difficult to say much about Egyptian occupation here since, apart from the temples, no traces of New Kingdom activity have been found. We do not know exactly when the Egyptians reached the Gebel Barkal area, but an inscription of Tuthmosis III is the first certain evidence for their presence. In this inscription Tuthmosis speaks of the 'Holy Mountain', which must surely mean Gebel Barkal, and says that a fort had been established there, though no trace of a fort has been found. Although the site of the town founded by the Egyptians, or perhaps taken over from the Nubians, is not known there seems little doubt but that there was a walled town here. In an inscription on the temple at Amada Amenophis II says that he hanged one of his Asiatic enemies from the top of the town wall, and in the Tuthmosis III inscription the fort is named 'Slayer of the Foreigners'.

Important information on the nature of Egyptian relations with Nubia is in the representations in the tomb of Huy at Thebes. Huy had been governor of Nubia during the reign of Tutankhamen and had built a walled town and a temple at Faras, which was badly damaged in much later times, with many of the blocks being found in the Meroitic cemetery. His tomb shows scenes of his appointment as governor as well as scenes of Nubians bringing tribute. These scenes not only are important for showing the products of the southern lands but also throw light on the nature of life in Nubia. It has been pointed out by several writers that there is a marked difference in the dress worn by the Nubians bringing tribute in this tomb compared with those depicted some hundred years earlier in the tomb of Rekhmire, a very high official in the reign of Tuthmosis III. In the earlier tomb the Nubians are wearing simple loin cloths whilst those in the later tomb are dressed in Egyptian-style clothing. This has been taken to show the way in which the Nubians had become adjusted to an Egyptian style of life, although the facial appearance of both the groups is similar. Certainly there is evidence for some Nubians having acquired many Egyptian characteristics. This is shown in two tombs at Debeira, a short way downstream of the second cataract. At Debeira East a local Nubian chief with the Egyptian name of Djehuty-hetep made a rock-cut tomb of Egyptian style with tomb paintings showing typically Egyptian paintings of hunting, feasting, and inspecting an estate containing date and dom palms which is being worked on by two different groups. These agricultural workers have skins of two different shades. One group are black, perhaps slaves from further south, whilst the others are shown as brown-skinned and perhaps represent the native people of Lower Nubia, descendants of the C-Group.

There is more evidence for the Egyptianization of at least the upper classes of Nubia since Djehuty-hetep's brother Amenemhet also built a tomb of Egyptian style on the other side of the river. Somewhat later Heka-nefer, prince of Miam (Aniba), who is shown as an important Nubian ruler in the

Figure 24.   Scene from tomb of Djehuty-hetep
(from T. Säve-Söderbergh, *Kush* XI, 1963)

tomb of Huy at Thebes, was also buried in an Egyptian-style tomb. Huy was governor of Nubia in the reign of Tutankhamen.

Evidence for the life and culture of the native inhabitants, other than the few nobles already referred to, is based almost entirely on burials and we know of no traces of their dwellings. These people continued to be buried in graves similar to those of the C-Group and Kerma people, and there can be little doubt that they were basically the same Nubian population who have lived in Nubia for many hundreds of years, but perhaps now with a greater admixture of darker people from further south. In Lower Nubia there are many graves of Nubian type for at least the early part of the eighteenth dynasty, but they gradually became Egyptianized as time went on and this is perhaps to be seen as another example of acculturation of the indigenous population. Some of the latest C-Group graves contain only Egyptian pottery, suggesting very strongly that the Nubians were eager to adopt Egyptian goods even if they continued to be buried in a traditional way.

It has also been noted that the number of graves, both Nubian and Egyptian, decreases by the late eighteenth dynasty and there seems to have been a reduction in population from the 15,000 to 20,000 which has been suggested for Lower Nubia in the early New Kingdom. The reasons for this are not clear, but it has been suggested that many Nubians withdrew to Upper Egypt, and that with a decrease in the Nile floods agricultural land became scarce, leading to withdrawal of both Nubians and Egyptians. Evidence for the native population and its graves comes almost entirely from Lower Nubia and little archaeological work has been done in Upper Nubia to investigate aspects of native life.

A group of people who come into some prominence during the period of the New Kingdom occupation are the Medjay. They are usually identified with those buried in the 'Pan-Graves' (already referred to in chapter 4). Known by name from the late Old Kingdom and certainly resident in the eastern desert, they are usually, because of their location and the supposed similarity of their name, assumed to be the predecessors of the present day Bega people of the Red Sea hills.

It seems that from Old Kingdom times they took service with the Egyptians, and Weni, an Egyptian official of the sixth dynasty, included them in an army which he led against eastern enemies of Egypt. They also appear as mercenaries in the troubled times of the First Intermediate period along with Nubians, from whom they are clearly distinguished.

During the New Kingdom the Medjay became prominent as part of the army and were employed widely as police so that the name Medjay came to be used to identify this police force. A shrine to the god Horus and to the deified Sesostris III near to that of Hekanefer at Toshka bears, as its maker, the name of Humay who is described in a hieroglyphic text as 'the Medjay of his majesty'. He carries a bow and arrow and was presumably a local military commander. The presence of typical Pan-Grave sherds close to the shrine presumably means that it was a place of worship for locally based Medjay troops. This is an example of how some aspects of Egyptian culture and religion had been adopted, at least by the commanders, whilst the rank and file were still using their traditional pottery and probably still living in a traditional way.

By the nineteenth dynasty there seems to have been little occasion for military activity by the Egyptians in a peaceful Nile valley and there is nothing to suggest military activity anywhere in Wawat, which by this time must have been heavily Egyptianized, nor in Kush, which had many Egyptian settlers. Depictions of Egyptian victories over southerners are likely to be boastful claims to enhance reputation rather than true representations of events. Horemheb is shown in a rock-cut chapel near the sandstone quarries at Silsila, north of Aswan, as returning from a campaign in Nubia, but this is usually taken to represent a visit by the Pharaoh of a ceremonial nature to demonstrate that after the confused period of the reign of Akhenaten and his immediate successors Egyptian rule was back to normal. There are further depictions of Egyptian victories over southerners and Seti I left at Sai an inscription describing a campaign in Irem. There has been considerable discussion as to the location of Irem but it is clear that it was not anywhere in the Nile valley downstream of the fourth cataract. It must have lain further south or west and it has been suggested that it may have been beyond the fifth cataract.

It was inevitable that Ramesses II, responsible for more monuments that any other pharaoh, should have left his mark on Nubia, and within the confines of Lower Nubia are a number of temples from his time. These temples are substantially different from earlier ones, which were in the main free-standing and often built within the towns established by the Egyptian colonizers, though Horemheb, as described above, had already shown that the cliffs of Nubia were suitable for cave-like structures. They were usually rock-cut, with the largest and most famous example being Abu Simbel, although this was not always so; Ramesses II had at least one free-standing temple built at Aksha. The Abu Simbel temple – whose dismemberment and re-erection in the 1960s clear of the lake formed by the High Dam at Aswan was one of the great triumphs of the international campaign to save the monuments of Nubia – though certainly completed by Ramesses II, may have been started by Seti I since an inscription of the first year of Ramesses II implies that much of the excavation of the vast cave which forms the temple must have been completed by that year (Plate 19a).

The temple was dedicated to the gods Re-Harakhte, the sun god, Amun, the national god and to Ramesses II himself. It is carefully sited so that twice a year, for a few days in February and October, the early morning sun lights up the innermost sanctuary with statues of Ramesses which form the façade. Two on either side flank the entrance to the chambers which form the temple. Standing beside these figures and much smaller are figures of members of the royal family – his wife Nefertari, the queen mother Muttuy and several of his children. On the sides of the thrones on which the colossal figures sit are shown captured prisoners from Asia and Africa and on the knee of the second colossus from the south are the interesting Greek graffiti carved by mercenary soldiers of Psammetichus II when he invaded Nubia in 591 BC. At the south end of the terrace which runs along in front of the colossi is the marriage stela which commemorates the arranged marriage between Ramesses and a daughter of the Hittite king Hattusilis II.

Inside the entrance in the main hall are two rows of four square pillars each with a statue of the Pharaoh in the form of Osiris and the pillars and the walls of this room are covered with relief sculpture showing religious ceremonies and the military exploits of the king in Syria, where one of his favourite themes, the battle of Kadesh, is shown, as well as victories, perhaps fictional, over Nubians. This room leads to a smaller hall with four columns which opens into the sanctuary. This chamber contains seated statues, representing Re-Harakhte, Amun, Ptah and the pharaoh, which have been carved out of the rock of the west wall.

A little way to the north is another smaller rock-cut temple which is dedicated to the goddess Hathor and to Queen Nefertari. This temple is considerably smaller than that of the pharaoh, but is still impressive, and has on either side of the entrance three colossi 11.5 metres high. Of the three the two on either side are of Ramesses and the one in the middle of Nefertari. Within the interior chamber, which has six Hathor-headed pillars, are scenes mainly of Ramesses either killing enemies, both Asiatic and Nubian, or making offerings to the gods, and, at the far west end within a recess, there is a statue of Hathor in the form of a cow protecting the Pharaoh.

There are several other rock-cut temples of this period. Going from north to south the first was at Beit el Wali, a temple which has been moved and re-erected near to Aswan. This temple is only partly cut into the rock and has an open forecourt. It has lively scenes of the pharaoh's wars against both Asiatic and Nubian enemies as well as illustrations of Nubian tribute. The next temple is at Gerf Hussein and was built late in Ramesses's reign, in the time of the governor Setaw, whom we know to have been the last to serve under Ramesses II. Wadi el Sebua was approached by a line of sphinxes and also had an open court in front of the rock-cut inner hall and sanctuary, where there are statues of the gods Amun, Ra-Harakhti and Ramesses himself. There are battle scenes here which closely resemble those at Beit el Wali. The last of these temples is at Derr where the temple was dedicated, like Abu Simbel, to Re-Harakhte, Amun, Ptah and Ramesses. This temple resembles that of Abu Simbel, but is smaller and lacks the colossi. It also contains scenes showing Ramesses's Nubian victories. This temple has also been removed from its original position and been re-erected close to the shore of the new lake.

Ramesses II certainly depicted military victories against the people of Nubia but it has been much doubted whether these events actually took place. It had become traditional for the pharaohs to claim such victories and the artists may have been merely carrying on what had become a boastful custom and claiming imaginary events that contributed to the glorification of the pharaoh. There can be no certainty that Ramesses did not campaign in Nubia; he certainly did in Asia. There seems little doubt that Seti I had campaigned to the south of Egypt, and it may be that Ramesses also found it necessary to lead troops, or perhaps to have them led by his generals, against tribes on the fringes. After the reign of Ramesses II the evidence for Egyptian activity in Nubia is much reduced, and it seems that there was also a decrease in population. Nubians figure prominently in the Egyptian army of Ramesses III (1198–1166 BC), when an officer of Nubian archers was involved in a palace conspiracy against the pharaoh.

There are traces of an Egyptian presence. The name of Ramesses III is found at Semna; a governor of Wawat named Pennut erected a statue of Ramesses VI (1156–1148 BC) in the temple at Derr, though this would be close to the end of effective Egyptian rule. The governor of Kush then was Penehesi, whose name, 'the Nehesi' strongly suggests that he was of local origin, as the word Nehesi was used as a term for some of the people of Nubia from at least as early as 2,000 BC. He led his own troops into Upper Egypt to oppose invading Libyans but withdrew to Kush after being defeated by the Libyans who had established their rule over Upper Egypt under Herihor (c.1000 BC). Herihor took the titles of pharaoh and of governor of Kush, but did not exercise anything other than nominal control, even over Wawat. It has been suggested that the name of an otherwise unknown king, Men-Ra-sehetep-en-Amun, found in the temple at Gebel Barkal, may be of the twenty-first dynasty, and, if so, that inscription implies that there was some pharaonic activity. This virtually marks the end of Egyptian power and we have no information as to the nature of Egyptian withdrawal. We do not know if Egyptian settlers, landowners and the priests of the various temples stayed on to become absorbed gradually into the local population, or whether they made a formal withdrawal into Egypt.

By about 1100 BC nearly all traces of the pharaoh's domination was gone. Lower Nubia seems to have been largely abandoned both by Egyptians and Nubians, or so the absence of archaeological traces, whether of dwellings or cemeteries, suggests, although the Pharaoh Shoshenq I (945–924 BC) of the twenty-second dynasty probably invaded Lower Nubia on at least one occasion. The reason for this abandonment may have been a drop in the Nile levels which made it difficult to continue agriculture when there was no effective means of raising the water high enough to irrigate land previously cultivated. As already suggested, one can presume that the Egyptians went back to Egypt, but what happened to the indigenous inhabitants is much less clear. It has been suggested that they withdrew to Upper Egypt but there is no certain evidence of this, nor does archaeology tell us the answer.

CHAPTER 6

THE GROWTH OF AN INDEPENDENT SUDANESE STATE; NAPATA AND MEROE

———————◆———————

By the end of Ramesside times Egyptian control over Nubia had virtually ceased and this must be attributed to a weakening of central power. Some inscriptions of the many pharaohs bearing the name of Ramesses have been found in Lower Nubia, but further up stream the towns and temples founded by the Egyptians in the period after 1500 BC seem to have been abandoned and Egyptian troops and officials withdrawn, as discussed in the previous chapter.

Archaeological evidence for the events of the time is largely negative and there is little to show of either Egyptians or indigenous Nubians. In earlier times the C-Group left plentiful evidence of their occupation of the Nile Valley, so it is strange to find so little trace of human occupation for the few hundred years between the withdrawal of the Egyptians and the beginning of a native dynasty. This may be due to the accident of discovery, but in view of the amount of archaeological work done in Lower Nubia it seems unlikely that a substantial population would have left so little trace of their presence and it must be supposed that there was a considerable decrease of population. This, as on other similar occasions, may have been due to changes in river level and reduction in the amount of cultivable land.

Whatever the situation during the first two hundred years or so after the withdrawal of the Egyptians from both Upper and Lower Nubia, there is a gap in the archaeological and historical evidence until, in about 850 BC, the first burials are found of an indigenous ruling family based in the town of Napata and the sacred area around Gebel Barkal. In earlier times, the Egyptians had built a temple close to the hill, as described in the previous chapter, which from its imposing appearance in an otherwise flat landscape had become an object of veneration (Plates 18b, 23). There had been a town of importance at this place, though whether it was an Egyptian foundation or

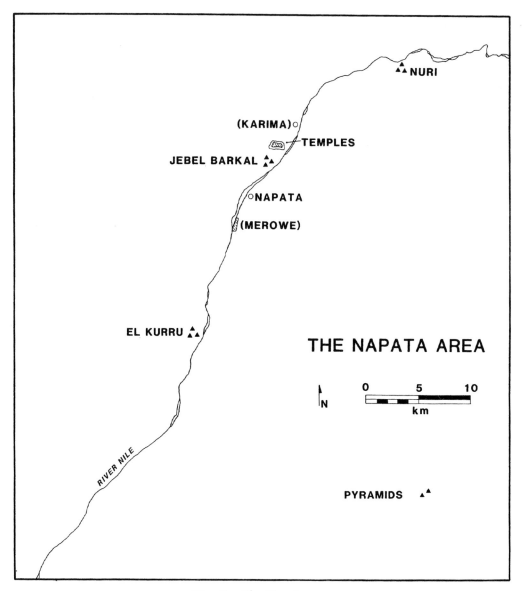

Map 7. The Napata area

whether the Egyptians moved into a Nubian settlement is uncertain. The first mention of Napata is of the time of the pharaoh Amenophis II, as described in the previous chapter, when he claimed to have hanged the body of a Syrian rebel on the town wall. The exact site of the town is not known and it may have been on either the right or the left bank of the river.

The burials, under mounds of sand and gravel at Kurru, twenty kilometres downstream from Gebel Barkal, are in a cemetery where a subsequent line of rulers was buried and seem to be those of important personages, very probably chiefs of much of Upper Nubia, whose descendants we know as the kings of Napata. No names are known for those buried in the mound graves but after five or six generations, represented by thirteen graves and covering a period of a hundred years or more, a more elaborate style of burial under rectangular sandstone constructions (known to archaeologists as 'mastabas' from the Arabic word meaning a bench) were developed. In one of these was buried Kashta, the first of the local rulers whose name is known for certain, though later inscriptions give the name of Alara as a predecessor. He may have been a brother of Kashta. Although Reisner, the American excavator of the Kurru cemetery, thought these were alien rulers, this view has now been abandoned and there is little doubt that those buried here were members of a native African dynasty whose forerunners, even if not direct

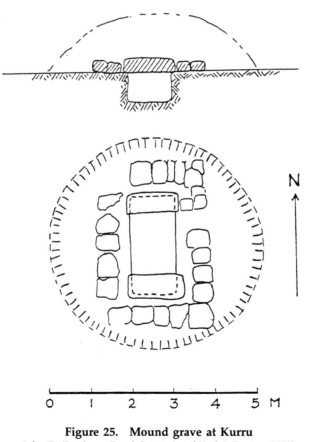

Figure 25. Mound grave at Kurru
(*after* D. Dunham, *Royal Cemeteries of Kush* I, Boston, 1950)

97

ancestors, were at Kerma. Although there is little direct archaeological evidence to connect the people of the Kurru cemetery with those of Kerma, the tradition of burial under mounds and the laying of the corpse on a bed goes back to that time, and some pottery found at Kurru has a resemblance to that of Kerma and of the C-Group, described in earlier chapters. Although there is a considerable time gap between the latest manifestations of Kerma and C-Group cultures and the burials at Kurru – perhaps 600 years – such gaps are not unknown in the archaeology of the Sudan and may well be filled as further field work, particularly in the Dongola reach, is carried out.

What connections these rulers had with Egypt is not very clear. It is certain that Egyptian military rule had been ended for some time but the presence of much Egyptian material in the graves, of which a gold nugget with an inscription in Egyptian hieroglyphs is the best known, suggests that there were at least commercial contacts. There may have been more than that, and the continued use of Egyptian language and writing suggests that groups of Egyptians, perhaps priests of the temple at Gebel Barkal, may have stayed on after the withdrawal of Egyptian control and acted as a focus for a continuation of Egyptian culture. Even if this is so, there is no doubt that the rulers were not Egyptians and the nature of the burial customs is clear evidence for this.

King Kashta may have gone to Thebes (modern Luxor) in Egypt, which had been the capital of Egypt for several centuries, and he certainly took the title of King of Upper and Lower Egypt, as can be seen in a stela fragment from Elephantine, thus claiming to be the ruler of that country, but there is no suggestion of a military campaign or that the claim to rule was more than an unsubstantiated and boastful one. The first of the Napatan kings known for certain to have ruled in Egypt was Piankhy, son of Kashta, (it is now

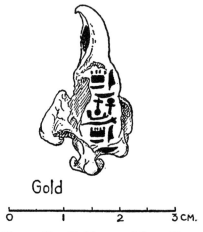

Gold

0   1   2   3 CM.

Figure 26.   Gold nugget from Kurru
(after D. Dunham, *Royal Cemeteries of Kush* I, Boston, 1950)

generally considered that his name should be read as Piye, but since much of the literature knows him as Piankhy that name is retained). Piankhy is regarded as the first king of the Egyptian twenty-fifth dynasty. His burial place at Kurru is known and details of his invasion of Egypt are given in an inscription on a granite stela, written in Egyptian hieroglyphs, which was found at Gebel Barkal in 1862 and removed to Cairo.

Under Kashta there may have been some acknowledgement of Napatan rule in Egypt, probably based on the close association of the Napatan rulers with the worship of Amun and other gods of Thebes. Piankhy, after an uneventful twenty years as ruler of Napata from c.751 BC, was faced with a different situation when the rather tenuous connection with Egypt was threatened by the advance from Lower Egypt of a prince Tefnakhte towards Thebes. Piankhy led an army northwards, reached Thebes – where he demonstrated his piety and support for the cult of Amun by participating in various temple rituals – and then moved on to Hermopolis (modern Eshmunein in middle Egypt) where he captured the town and its ruler, Namlot, and expressed his anger at the bad treatment that Namlot's horses had received. This concern with horses seems to have been a characteristic of several Napatan kings, and in the Kurru cemetery there are formal burials of twenty-four horses, probably representing twelve teams of the two necessary to draw chariots. Four of these horses probably date from the reign of Piankhy and others are firmly associated with some of his successors. In addition to the description of the campaign given in the Gebel Barkal stela Piankhy also recorded details of his campaign in reliefs, now very much damaged, in the second court of the Barkal temple. The two outer courts of this temple were added by Piankhy and have recently been re-studied.

Piankhy was succeeded by his younger brother, Shabako, whose claim to have suppressed a revolt in Egypt is recorded on a commemorative scarab, and then by his son Shebitku, both of whom seem to have lived mostly in Egypt, probably at Memphis. They erected a number of buildings in Egypt, especially at Karnak, though they were buried in the family cemetery at Kurru. The next ruler was Taharqa, nephew of Shabako and the best known of the kings of Napata. He left many monuments, both in Egypt and Nubia, of which the best known is a colonnade in the first court of the temple of Amun at Karnak of which one column has been re-erected. He also left evidence for at least some Napatan occupation of Lower Nubia on inscribed stone blocks at the fortress hill of Qasr Ibrim, as well as at Buhen and Semna. He also built a large temple at Kawa in Upper Nubia where historical inscriptions give information concerning his reign, and also give a vivid account of a heavy downpour of rain and its effect on the environment and the temple.

Taharqa became ruler in c.690 BC and seems to have spent much of the early years of his reign in Egypt having been crowned in Memphis. He was increasingly troubled by Assyrian attempts to drive him out of Egypt, including a severe defeat in 671 BC when Esarhaddon of Assyria forced him out of Memphis, leaving his wife and a son behind. It was not until the reign of his nephew, Tanwetamani, that the Assyrians finally succeeded in defeating the Napatan forces, and in 663 BC they sacked the city of Thebes – an event which was recorded in the Bible in the description by the prophet Nahum (3: 8–10). This event marked the end of Napatan rule in Egypt, and from this time on the kings remained within the boundaries of their own territory in Nubia.

Unfortunately the town of Napata has not been identified and though temples have been found on both sides of the river, there is no trace of domestic occupation. Remains of what may have been a palace and of store rooms suggests that the royal residence and the town of Napata may have been on the left bank,and that the area around Gebel Barkal on the other side of the river may have been reserved for the service of the gods. The presence of a great temple, and others discovered more recently by an Italian expedition, strongly suggests that this was so. A recent discovery, by an expedition from the Museum of Fine Arts in Boston led by Dr T. Kendall, has shown that the famous hill of Gebel Barkal, below which lies the Amun temple, had a semi-detached pinnacle previously thought to have been a colossal statue but now known not to be. This pinnacle contains a small shrine cut into the rock which may have contained a statue of Taharqa and above it was found evidence that inscriptions with the name of Taharqa, and of King Nastasen (who lived three hundred years later), were carved in the rock and that a metal sheet, which the finder considers must have been of gold, was fixed there. Dr Kendall also suggests that the very noticeable pinnacle was regarded as a gigantic representation of the Uraeus, the cobra-head symbol of Egyptian royalty which was adopted by the rulers of Kush.

The development of a strong Egyptian influence in the culture of the Napatans is seen most clearly in the royal burial customs. Starting with a typically Nubian burial style the early rulers were buried under mounds with the bodies laid on a bed, similar to the *angareeb*, the standard bed of the Sudan today, made of a wooden framework and a mattress of rope. The next stage was the use of mastabas to cover the burials, and then the kings were buried under pyramids which are, in their size and sharply pointed angle, certainly derived from those in use by private persons in the New Kingdom, as seen at Deir el Medina at Thebes and, in Nubia, at Aniba. At these places they were not used for royal burials but for those of important non-royal personages.

The first king to be buried under a pyramid was probably Piankhy, though the destruction of the superstructure of his burial place makes it difficult to be certain that it was a pyramid and not a mastaba. A pyramid is likely and the later kings certainly seem to have been placed in tombs cut into rock under small pyramids. From this time on, at various places, all Napatan and subsequently all Meroitic royal burials were under pyramids and the bed burials of earlier times were replaced by the use of wooden coffins and in some cases of stone sarcophagi.

Other examples of Egyptian influence can be seen in the use of the Egyptian language, written in hieroglyphs, for royal inscriptions, though it is unlikely that Egyptian was the spoken tongue. Temples closely followed the patterns of Egyptian ones and were used for the worship of Egyptian gods, of whom Amun was the most important. A range of objects of Egyptian design have been found in the tombs. These may have been imported from Egypt or made locally either by groups of expatriate Egyptians or by local craftsmen trained to copy Egyptian styles. Since the earlier burials at Kurru are of Nubian style and it is only from the time of Piankhy that Egyptian ones begin to dominate, it can be supposed that it was the close connection with Egypt arising after Piankhy's invasion that was responsible for the change.

Taharqa was buried in c.664 BC under a pyramid (Plate 24a) in a new cemetery on the opposite side of the river to Kurru, and about 22 kilometres further upstream. This new cemetery, known from the nearby modern village as Nuri, then became the burial place for twenty succeeding rulers from c.650 BC to c.290 BC. Although Taharqa's pyramid at Nuri marks the start of the use of this cemetery, his immediate successor, Tanwetamani, was buried at Kurru as the last of the kings of Egypt's twenty-fifth dynasty, although in c.350 BC one more king whose name is not known was buried there.

There has been some discussion as to whether Taharqa was buried at Nuri, or whether the pyramid which bears his name was perhaps a cenotaph. The argument for this is based on the finding of a group of badly damaged pyramids in a large Meroitic cemetery at Sedenga, much further north, where in one of them blocks with reliefs of a royal figure resembling Taharqa and parts of his royal titulary were found. The relative insignificance of this group of pyramids, the majority of which are of much later date, makes it more likely that the blocks with the king's name are re-used and came from a temple, now destroyed, which had been built by Taharqa.

The twenty post-Taharqa burials at Nuri are all under pyramids (Plate 24b) and the names of the kings buried there are known from inscriptions on objects, mainly the figures of Egyptian style known as *shawabtis* found in the tombs. After Taharqa, the Napatan kings never set foot in Egypt, but maintained a fiction of Egyptian kingship by using the titulary of the pharaohs. Of these kings some have left details of their activities in inscriptions written in Egyptian hieroglyphs. Anlamani records a visit to the temple of Kawa. A temple (B 700) close to the main Amun temple at Gebel Barkal was started in the reign of Atlanersa and finished by his successor Senkamanisken.

Aspelta, in two stelae found at Gebel Barkal, records details of his accession and of the method by which he was selected to be king. In his reign the Egyptian pharaoh Psammetichus II invaded Nubia and may have reached and sacked Napata in 591 BC.

Following Aspelta, who died c.560 BC, there is no information until the time of Amani-nete-yerike (c.431–405 BC) of whom there are inscriptions in the temple of Kawa, built by Taharqa. The main inscription gives some information as to events; it records military campaigns, gives details of his accession ceremony and describes a visit to Kawa, where repairs and cleaning were carried out in the temple, and it contains the first mention of the town of Meroe. Harsiotef and Nastasen have inscriptions from Gebel Barkal dealing largely with military events and, in the case of Nastasen, a description of his journey across the Bayuda desert from Meroe to Napata to be accepted as king in the Amun temple at Gebel Barkal, presumptive evidence that Meroe was by that time, if not earlier, the royal residence.

In about 310 BC Nastasen was the last king to be buried at Nuri; the pyramid of his successor Arakamani is at Meroe. From this time on, with all the royal burials at Meroe, there is little doubt that city had become the centre of the state which can now be called Meroitic. At what time the kings moved their residence from Napata is not certain, but the beginning of royal burials certainly marks an important change in the nature of the Meroitic kingship. The town of Meroe had been occupied from much earlier and excavations there suggest that it may have existed in the eighth century BC. The fact of royal burials at Kurru and Nuri and the known importance of Napata and its many temples strongly implies that it was the centre of the state in the time of the first rulers of Kush, but we know that even whilst burials were still in the Napata area kings were living at Meroe and this suggests that the royal residence was transferred there long before burials under the Meroe pyramids began.

The history of Nubia during the time of the Napatan kings is based almost entirely on a study of royal burials and temples, and there is very little other archaeological material to give a more complete picture of the life of the time. Settlements have not been found and the only place where it is possible to see some of the indigenous material of the time is in the cemetery at Sanam. Here the burials fall into three different groups: the first being that in which the bodies were mummified and Egyptian or Egyptian-style objects were placed in brick-built chamber graves; the second contained extended burials in rectangular pits with Egyptian types of pottery; the third had contracted burials and contained, along with Egyptian pottery, vessels reminiscent of those of C-Group and Kerma times. This variation of burial types has suggested either class distinctions, with those buried in the Egyptian manner belonging to an Egyptianized upper class, or possibly an ethnic difference with the third type of burial being of the indigenous population whilst the others represent those of Egyptians who may have remained behind after the withdrawal of Egyptian administration and acted as priests of Amun, as scribes who kept the knowledge of Egyptian writing, and as craftsmen who manufactured the large number of Egyptian objects which have been found.

Away from the main centre of Napata virtually nothing is known of Napatan times other than the temples. Towns and villages there must have been, the town of Meroe existed and at Kawa certainly there are the remains of a large town still awaiting investigation. Emphasis on the major monuments – temples at Kawa, Sanam and Gebel Barkal – has meant that there has been little work done on searching for villages and cemeteries of commoners and it has been suggested that much of Nubia was depopulated at the time. Though a drop in river level may have meant a drop in population in Lower Nubia, the presence of temples, some towns and royal burials in Upper Nubia suggests that there must have been sufficient population to provide the labour force for building and for the agricultural production necessary for the maintenance of those concerned with the royal court and the temple priesthood. Even though their remains have not been found, the ordinary folk of Napatan times must have been living in village settlements with houses of either mud brick or matting, and it is only the very scanty remains which they will have left behind which has prevented them being found. The finding of a cemetery of Napatan times at Missimina, well north of the third cataract, shows that there was occupation there and although the settlement has not been found, the presence of the cemetery goes some way to modify views of the depopulation of the area.

What little evidence there is, largely from the cemetery of Sanam, suggests that there had been a steady continuum of indigenous culture throughout the 500 years of pharaonic rule stemming from the better known peoples of the Kerma and C-Group cultures. The resemblance of the non-Egyptian ceramics at Sanam to these earlier ones, and its re-appearance in even later times, strongly suggests that throughout a very long time there had been a native culture represented now by scanty finds of pottery. Most of the other artifacts would have been of perishable materials – wood, leather, basketry and gourd – whilst the Egyptians, or those richer Nubians with access to Egyptian goods, were able to acquire objects made in less perishable materials and thus give a one-sided picture of the culture of the time.

The move of the royal burial place from Napata to Meroe at some time about 300 BC is usually taken to mark the beginning of the Meroitic period and it certainly is reflected in changes in cultural and artistic production. It may not be coincidence that this date is close to that of the invasion of Egypt by Alexander the Great in 332 BC; certainly the subsequent influence of Greek art and culture in Egypt is reflected in the Meroitic kingdom.

Table 2 List of Kushite rulers, burial places and approximate assumed dates

1.	Kashta	Ku.8	760–751 BC
2.	Piankhy	Ku.17	751–716
3.	Shabako	Ku.15	716–701
4.	Shebitku	Ku.18	701–690
5.	Taharqa	Nu.1	690–664
6.	Tanwetamani	Ku.16	664–653
7.	Atlanersa	Nu.20	653–643
8.	Senkamanisken	Nu.3	643–623
9.	Anlamani	Nu.6	623–593
10.	Aspelta	Nu.8	593–568
11.	Amtalqa	Nu.9	568–555
12.	Malenaqen	Nu.5	555–542
13.	Analmaye	Nu.18	542–538
14.	Amani-nataki-lebte	Nu.10	538–519
15.	Karkamani	Nu.7	519–510
16.	Amaniastabarqa	Nu.2	510–487
17.	Siaspiqa	Nu.4	487–468
18.	Nasakhma	Nu.19	468–463
19.	Malewiebamani	Nu.11	463–435
20.	Talakhamani	Nu.16	435–431
21.	Amani-nete-yerike	Nu.12	431–405
22.	Baskakeren	Nu.17	405–404
23.	Harsiotef	Nu.13	404–369
24.	?	Ku.1	369–350
25.	Akhratan	Nu.14	350–335
26.	Nastasen	Nu.15	335–310
27.	Amanibakhi ?	Nu.?	310–295
28.	Arakakamani	Beg.S.6	295–275
29.	Amanislo	Beg.S.5	275–260
30.	Bartare	Beg.S.10	260–250
31.	Amani..tekha ?	Beg.N.4	250–235
32.	(Arnekhamani)	Beg.N.53	235–218
33.	Arqamani	Beg.N.7	218–200
34.	Tabirqa ?	Beg.N.9	200–185
35.	. . . iwal ?	Beg.N.8	185–170
36.	Shanakdakhete)	Beg.N.11	170–160
37.	?	Beg.N.12	160–145
38.	(Naqrinsan) ?	Beg.N.13	145–120
39.	((Tanyidamani))	Beg.N.20	120–100
40.	((. . . khale))	Beg.N.21	100–80
41.	((..amani)) ?	Beg.N.14	80–65
42.	(Amanikhabale)	Beg.N.2	65–41
43.	Amanishakhete	Beg.N.6	41–12
44.	Netekamani	Beg.N.2	12BC-AD12
45.	Amanitare	Beg.N.1	12BC-AD12
46.	(Sherkarer)	Beg.N.10	AD12–17
47.	((Pisakar))	Beg.N.15	17–35
48.	Amanitaraqide	Beg.N.16	35–45
49.	Amanitenmemide	Beg.N.17	45–62
50.	Amanikhatashan	Beg.N.18	62–85
51.	Tarekeniwal	Beg.N.19	85–103
52.	((Amanikhalika))	Beg.N.32	103–108

53.	(Aritenyesbekhe)	Beg.N.34	108–132
54.	((Aqrakamani))	Beg.N.40	132–137
55.	((Adeqetali))	Beg.N.41	137–146
56.	Takideamani	Beg.N.29	146–165
57.	((..reqerem))??	Beg.N.30	165–184
58.	. . .	Beg.N.37	184–194
59.	((Teritedakhatey))	Beg.N.38	194–209
60.	Aryesbekhe	Beg.N.36	209–228
61.	Teritnide	Beg.N.51	228–246
62.	Aretnide	Beg.N.35	246
63.	Teqeredeamani	Beg.N.28	246–266
64.	((Tamelerdeamani))?	Beg.N.27	266–283
65.	((Yesbekhamani))?	Beg.N.24	283–300
66.	((Lakhideamani))?	Beg.N.26	300–308
67.	((Maleqerebar))?	Beg.N.25	308–320

Ku.=Kurru; Nu.=Nuri; Beg.=Begarawiya
? means reading of name uncertain;
() means identification with a tomb uncertain but probable;
(()) means identification with a tomb is only a guess.

The change of royal burial place may reflect political events which we cannot discern and a loss of prestige by the priesthood of Amun at Gebel Barkal, who may have been transferred to the Amun temple at Meroe or replaced by southern-based priests.

The town of Meroe, as already described, had been occupied during the eighth century BC, and there are burials there from the time of Piankhy. The first royal name to be found there is that of Senkamanisken (c.643–623 BC) and the first mention of the town in a text is in that of Amani-nete-yerike at Kawa in the early part of the fifth century BC which tells us that the king resided there.

From the burials under pyramids at Meroe, often known, from the name of the modern village close to the remains of the ancient town, as Begarawiya and therefore designated as Beg. (the burials in the Kurru cemetery are designated Ku. and those at Nuri as Nu.), it is possible to compile a list of rulers from Arakakamani to the end of the known history of Meroe (Table 2). There are some variations in the list as given by different scholars, and different spellings of royal names are now in vogue, but some sixty-five or more burials of rulers can be identified, beginning with those at Kurru. In a number of cases individuals can be attributed to the tombs by the finding of their names either on objects in the tomb or in inscriptions on the tomb chapels. For others there is some doubt as to the precise identification of ruler with burial place, and in all cases the dates are highly speculative, as is the order of the rulers. The order, and there is no other means for achieving this, has been arrived at by a careful study of various archaeological clues by

Reisner, who in the 1920s investigated all the Kushite royal tombs. By a brilliant study in which he used the position in the cemetery, and changes in architectural styles as well as the tomb contents, to arrive at a logical order, he established the list more or less as we now have it, and though there may be changes as knowledge increases, the order proposed by Reisner has stood up well to over fifty years of use and criticism. Table 2 shows those buried at Meroe with suggested dates. The dates for the first kings, those known from Egyptian sources as the twenty-fifth dynasty, are reasonably certain, with a few minor variations by different authorities, but from the death of Tanwetamani onwards the order of rulers and their dates is speculative. The names of many are known and are given in the list.

From Atlanersa on there are no dates that can be fixed with certainty. Aspelta is thought to have been ruling at the time of the campaign of Pharaoh Psammetichus in 593 BC. Arqamani, if he is the Ergamenes described by the Greek writer Diodorus Siculus, would have been reigning between 285–205 BC since he is said to have been a contemporary of Ptolemy II and Ptolemy IV, and Teqerideamani, who if he is the same as one of the same name mentioned in an inscription at Philae, was reigning in AD 253. All the other dates, and even the allegedly fixed ones, have had doubt cast on them, are merely an attempt to fit the known rulers into the approximately known time span. The lengths of reign are adjusted according to pyramid size, assuming that the longer the reign the larger and more elaborate the pyramid and by the quantity and quality of the objects buried in the tombs. Even this criterion is uncertain since all the tombs had been robbed in the past and no longer give accurate information as to the original wealth of the deposits.

However that may be, and however uncertain the dates of individual rulers, the kings and, sometimes, queens of Meroe continued to rule from that town for many hundreds of years. The town was inhabited for at least 1,000 years, and controlled a state along the whole of the Nile valley from a short way south of Aswan, still then the Egyptian frontier town, to over 300 kilometres to the south of the capital at Meroe. Here there developed a distinct culture which we know as 'Meroitic'. Owing much to pharaonic and Ptolemaic Egyptian models, it developed a style with a marked flavour of its own. Many of the features which distinguish Meroitic from Napatan culture seem to start from about the time of the transference of the royal burials to Meroe, and, though it has now become the fashion to emphasize the continuity of Kushite culture, from this time there is a distinct change to be seen in formal sculpture on temples and tomb chapels and in the more mundane production of pottery.

It may be that there was a difference between the people of the south with Meroe as their centre and those, more susceptible to Egyptian influences, at Napata. Certainly Meroe was far better sited to develop as an important administrative and commercial centre. Napata stood in the narrow strip of cultivated land along the Nile with only desert as its hinterland. Meroe, on the other hand, lay in an area of annual rain with wide grazing land to the east and with the possibility not only of food production along the river banks but also in the large valleys which, during the rainy season flowed with water coming from the grassy plateau to the east. These, draining towards the Nile provided large areas for the growing of crops after the seasonal floods had passed.

Based on this favourable environment the town of Meroe developed into the largest one in the whole of Nubia, showing many of the characteristics of a well developed urban agglomeration with palaces, temples, many houses and some industry. Iron and pottery were produced in large quantity and

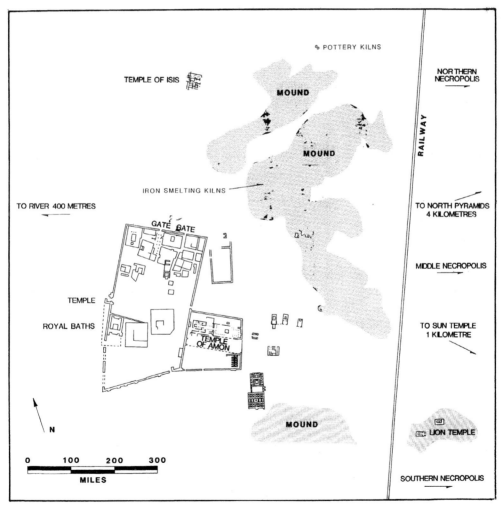

Map 8. Plan of Meroe town

there was also the manufacture of objects of copper, faience, ivory and glass and presumably of such perishable materials as wood, leather and cloth.

The town was well laid out (see Map 8) having distinct areas for the activities of royalty (palaces), priests (temples) and commoners (ordinary houses of sun-dried brick), as well as manufacturing areas sited so as to cause minimum pollution, at least to royalty, and with cemeteries, both royal and commoner, placed some way from the dwellings. It is these royal cemeteries which provided the information to compose the list of rulers given in Table 2. The cemeteries, consisting of pyramids with burial chambers below them, are found in three groups – the southern, northern and western cemeteries. The southern one lies on a spur separated by a small valley from the sandstone ridge on which the main northern cemetery was placed. It consists of more than two hundred graves of which the earliest date from the time of Piankhy. Many of these burials are simple pit burials and are of private persons, but there are also pyramid burials of members of the royal family, and the first rulers to be buried at Meroe (Arakakamani, Amanislo and Bartare) were placed there before the main burial ground for royalty was shifted to the ridge of the north cemetery. The west cemetery, on the plain slightly to the south-west of the other two, is considerably more ruined. It also consisted of pyramid burials, beginning with those contemporary with

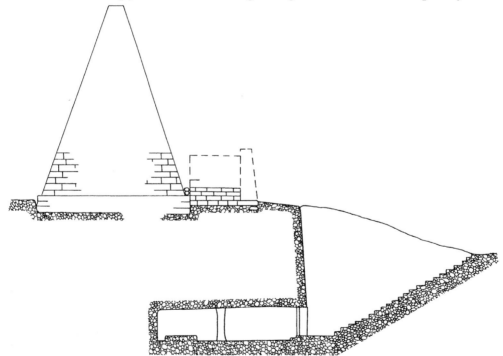

Figure 27. Section through Meriotic pyramid

the earliest ones of the south cemetery and lasting until the time of those in the north cemetery which represent the very latest royal burials. No graves of rulers have been found amongst the approximately five hundred graves of this cemetery, but the size of the superstructures and the elaborateness of the burial chambers and such of their contents as have survived centuries of robbing show that they are the burials of members of the royal family or of the upper classes.

Within the town the area known, with reason, as the royal palace is surrounded by a massive wall outside which is a temple to the god Amun, the largest Meroitic temple known and showing signs of re-building at various times – some of it certainly dates from the time of Netekamani and Amanitare, since their names were found on blocks in the small kiosk built on the main

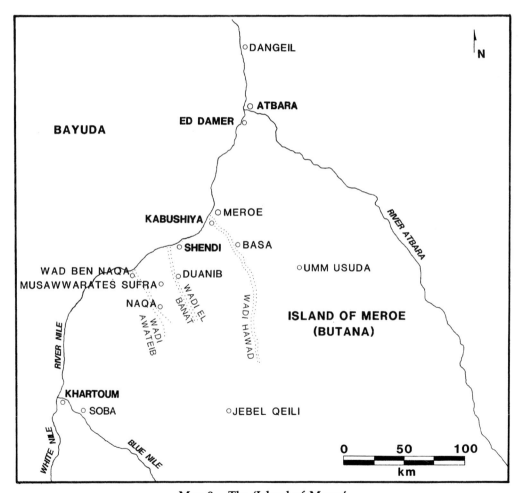

Map 9. The 'Island of Meroe'

axis of the outer court. The walls of this outer court have provided clear evidence for an earlier building, since blocks with relief sculpture have been built into the foundations.

The residential part of the town consists of rather small houses of sun-dried brick laid out in a regular pattern which continued to be the same for hundreds of years (Plate 27). On the very bottom level of excavation were found traces of post holes showing that some of the inhabitants were living in huts very similar to those used by some of the present-day inhabitants of the area. Iron-smelting furnaces have been found not far from the residential areas, and Meroe – though not perhaps, as used to be thought, the centre from which

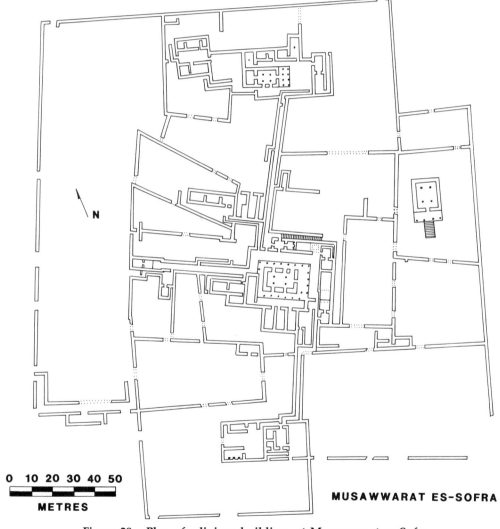

0 10 20 30 40 50
METRES

MUSAWWARAT ES-SOFRA

Figure 28. Plan of religious buildings at Musawwarat es Sofra

iron-working techniques spread throughout Africa – was certainly an important producer of iron from the fifth century BC or possibly earlier.

Away to the east in the ancient 'Island of Meroe', known today as the Keraba, there are two other important groups of monuments, both of them primarily of religious significance. Musawwarat es Sofra, perhaps the most remarkable group of buildings in Nubia, is something of a mystery. It consists of a series of walled enclosures surrounding a small temple built on a platform and reached by ramps – of which an unusual feature is a wall terminating in the form of an elephant and reconstructed from scattered fragments during the investigations from 1960 to 1968 by the Humboldt University of Berlin. The central temple can be dated on stylistic grounds to the first century AD or a little later, but excavation has shown that there were buildings here from as early as the fifth or sixth centuries BC. There are unfortunately no primary inscriptions to give a more accurate date, but there are many graffiti, mostly in the Meroitic language, but also in Egyptian demotic, Greek, Old Nubian and one in Latin.

The most informative discovery at this site was at what is known as the 'Lion Temple', since it was for the worship of the lion-headed Meroitic god, Apedemek, and lay a short distance from the 'Great Enclosure'. Before excavation this temple appeared only as a pile of rubble, but when the blocks were re-assembled, it was found that the sculptured reliefs and inscriptions on the south wall were almost intact, since this wall had collapsed outwards and the blocks had been preserved by lying face down in the sand. This temple is now known to have been erected by King Arnekhamani, and, since the inscriptions are in Egyptian, they can be read and comparison of the style of language, as well as of the hieroglyphs, with those known from Ptolemaic Egypt suggests that it was built in c.220 BC.

Some 18 kilometres to the south west, at Naqa, is another group of temples (Plate 25b). The site may well be that of an important town but although the standing monuments have been studied in detail, no excavations have been carried out, so information about it can only be derived from the group of temples. These consist of a temple to the lion-headed god Apedemek with most interesting reliefs of the time of Netekamani and Amanitare, here represented with Arikhankharer – who may, on the assumption that they were a couple, have been their son – worshipping a number of gods. This temple, from the depiction of known rulers, dates to somewhere in the late first century BC to the early first century AD. Close beside it is a temple of distinctive and unusual style showing very strong influence from Graeco-Roman Egypt and usually known as the 'Roman Kiosk'. It has been variously dated to either the third century AD or to the second half of the first century AD. There is also, on the lower slope of the hill which overlooks the site, a temple to the god Amun which contains inscriptions showing that it also was built in the time of Netekamani and therefore was contemporary with the Apedemek temple. At Wad ben Naqa, 75 kilometres up stream from Meroe, is another major site with a large building, probably a palace, with store rooms which, when excavated, contained quantities of timber, ivory and storage jars. Close beside it a beehive-shaped structure may have been for grain storage. There were at least two temples here, one with the names of Netekamani and Amanitare written in both Egyptian and Meroitic hiero-glyphs, and from this inscription the first clues were obtained for the reading of Meroitic inscriptions.

Other smaller Meroitic sites are scattered throughout the eastern part of the 'Island of Meroe', with a unique rock carving at Gebel Qeili, some way further south, of King Sherkarer defeating the enemy. Meroitic activity was widespread over the eastern Keraba, though much of it may have been nomadic and the only place that seems to have been a town of any size is at Naqa. A feature of the area is the presence of artificial reservoirs, *hafir* in Arabic, presumably to store water for the large herds of cattle which were grazed over the 'Island of Meroe'. Several of these had stone figures of lions, in one case a frog, placed round them to provide protection.

The most southerly site of the period so far known is at Sennar on the Blue Nile, where a settlement and cemetery have been found. It seems likely that other sites of this period may yet remain to be found in the area between the Blue and White Niles, and the site of Gebel Moya, not far from Sennar, although not itself representing Meroitic culture, shows that the people of the area were in touch with cultural manifestations from further north.

For this period of Nubian history the emphasis is on sites in the southern part of the Meroitic kingdom where the impact of the presence of royalty is seen in the large number of public buildings already described. In the north the population seems to have been sparse until late Meroitic times and little has been found earlier than the first century AD. The Dodecaschoinus, the region immediately up stream of Philae, was largely in Ptolemaic and sub-sequently Roman hands, and the most northerly Meroitic material comes from a cemetery at Garba.

Evidence of Meroitic activity can be deduced from inscriptions in some of the Ptolemaic temples, notably at Dakka where the name of Arqamani is found, perhaps indicating a short Meroitic occupation. South of Wadi el Sebua, Meroitic occupation becomes more common, and from the second century AD there was a considerable population at such places as Karanog and Qasr Ibrim. At Faras was a large settlement and cemetery, and here was the seat of the *pesate*, the governor of the northern, perhaps semi-independent, province of Akin. Over two thousand graves were excavated here, and the remains of a large official building, called the 'Western Palace' by the exca-vator, which may have been the residence of the governor, were found.

Signs of Meroitic occupation are found south of Faras, cemeteries being more commonly found than villages. At Amara there was a temple, now almost totally destroyed, though it was seen and recorded in the nineteenth century, once again of Netekamani and Amanitare – the most northerly record of these two well known rulers. At Sadenga there is a large cemetery of Meroitic pyramids and some earlier tombs re-used in Meroitic times. On the island of Argo, at Tabo (Plate 28b), another temple of perhaps the same date has been excavated and two colossal statues, probably of the gods Sebiumeker and Arensnuphis, known as standing on either side of temple entrances, have been moved to the Khartoum Museum. The next important site of the period is at Kawa, where temples and a town going back to New Kingdom times stand close to the river bank opposite the modern town of Dongola. The main temple building dates from the time of Taharqa, but additions were made by Harsiotef and other kings who were buried at Nuri, and some buildings and inscriptions date from the first century BC. In the town, only superficially examined as yet, occupation continued until the end of the third century AD when town and temples show signs of considerable fire damage.

At Gebel Barkal, where Napatan activities have already been described, there was considerable later building, and recent excavations have found a large complex from the time of Netekamani, probably a palace, not far from the well known temple complex.

THE ART

The art of later Kushite times, though having obvious links with that of Egypt, had, by the beginning of the third century BC developed sufficient distinctive features to be clearly distinguishable in style, though the themes, particularly of formal religious relief sculptures on temples, continued to draw heavily on Egyptian models. Good examples of such reliefs are to be seen on the walls of temples at Musawwarat es Sofra and Naqa, already described, and there are many others from the pyramid chapels of the royal cemeteries which lie fully within the Meroitic period and can be compared with the even more strongly Egyptian-style reliefs of the time of Taharqa at Kawa.

Sculpture in the round is less common. There is a series of royal statues of early kings, but, after the time of Aspelta, they are rather few. There are several examples of colossal statues, probably of the already mentioned gods Sebiumeker and Arensnuphis, which stood at the entrances of temples as at Argo, Musawwarat es Sofra and Meroe. A curious group of pieces comes from the so-called 'Roman bath' at Meroe, where a core of sandstone was built up in plaster which was then painted. Three small pieces, two certainly and the other probably from Meroe, are of special interest showing a number of details not otherwise known. The first shows King Tanyidamani (c.120–100 BC?) and the god Apedemek; the second, more crudely done, shows a king and a queen, not named, making offerings to Amun and to Isis – it may date from the first century AD; third, a fine piece shows Arikhankharer, known from Naqa, smiting his enemies in conventional pose, but with many unusual features including that of a winged protector behind his head. Many small pieces in other materials are known and there are some splendid examples of royal jewellery from burials of rulers, notably from that of Queen Amani-shakhete of the late first century BC.

The best known product of these times is the pottery, much of it ranking with the finest ceramics of the ancient world, and found in great quantity at the various sites that have been excavated. It falls into several different categories, ranging from a very fine painted, or sometimes stamped, ware, mainly used for small cups, and dating from the end of the fourth century BC – perhaps significantly near to the date of the first ruler to be buried at Meroe – to large storage jars often painted with a vine leaf motif. There are many other classes of household and kitchen pottery wares, showing a range of shapes and decoration, including a burnished black ware, often impressed and incised with white filling and copying the shapes of gourds. Some of these closely resemble the gourd vessels, known as *bukhsa*, used today in the western Sudan, which have a basketry neck and decorative wool tassels which the Meroitic potter carefully copied. This black pottery belongs to a tradition going back to C-Group times.

The art of the Kushites shows that a high level of sophistication had been reached, and Kush was certainly a civilization with a rich culture and one that was, on the evidence of many imported pieces from Egypt and the Mediterranean, in close contact with a wider world. It was also a literate civilization, and though early inscriptions and some later ones are in the Egyptian language and writing, the Meroites developed a writing system of their own in which they wrote in their own language. The twenty-three signs used in their writing are known in two forms: 'hieroglyphic' using, in modi-fied form, a small selection of Egyptian hieroglyphs, and 'cursive' an abbrevi-ated, though not properly cursive, form. The phonetic values of the signs have been discovered but the language of the inscriptions remains unknown, and only a very few words have been translated with any certainty. It is therefore not possible to use the large number of inscriptions to throw light on the life and history of the period, though items such as names, of both royalty and others, can be discerned, as well as official titles.

Of detailed history we have little information, except from the inscriptions of a few of the kings buried at Nuri, already referred to, until late in the first century BC when contacts between Meroe and the Roman Empire bring us

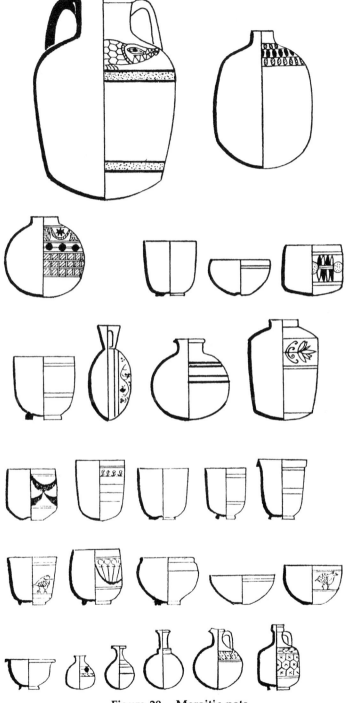

Figure 29.   Meroitic pots

some information, and classical writers provide a few details. In the fifth century BC Herodotus visited Egypt and ventured as far as Aswan, and gives some geographical description and other information of a rather mythological nature. After him there is no further mention of Nubia by historians until Diodorus Siculus, in the first century BC, who gives some details of the king Ergamenes. He is followed by Strabo, Pliny and Seneca and other classical writers. From these authors we learn of military activities, and an attack in 23 BC on Meroitic territory by Publius Petronius, the Roman governor of Egypt, probably as a counter to an earlier Meroitic attack on Aswan, during which it is possible that the famous head of Augustus, found at Meroe, was seized. It may be that Queen Amanishakhete, whose conventional dates (41–12 BC) span the period of the clash with Rome, was the ruler at this time, and she may have been the lady whose Meroitic title of *kandake* was referred to by Strabo. The exact meaning of the title is not known, but occurs several times with the names of royal ladies, and has been thought to be equivalent to 'queen', though it may not mean that the holder was a ruler unless the title *qere* is associated with it. Amanishakhete has both these titles and the size of her pyramid (Beg. N.6) and the splendid jewellery found in it shows that she was a person of great importance.

Shortly after this period of close, and hostile, contact with Rome – brought to an end by a treaty made with the Emperor Augustus at Samos – begins the greatest period of building activity, when Netekamani, frequently but not always associated with Amanitare, has his name on more monuments than any other Meroitic ruler. The amount of building shows that the first century AD was one of wealth and power in the Meroitic kingdom, but, after the early part of the century, we have very little information other than the names of rulers. The presence of imported objects in the tombs shows that commercial contact with Roman Egypt was maintained and there is plentiful archaeological evidence that the amount of Meroitic settlement in Lower Nubia was considerably increased, partly because of greater agricultural possibilities due to the introduction of the ox-driven water wheel, which was to become the mainstay of Nubian agriculture until modern times.

Some three centuries of peaceful development came to an end in about the middle of the fourth century AD, and though many details are obscure, the decline in the size and quality of royal burials and their contents strongly suggests an impoverishment and an end of the royal line by about this date.

The growing power of Axum, in Ethiopia, may have caused a decline in Meroe's commercial activities and an inscription by Ezana, King of Axum, dated to about AD 350, describes a military expedition into the 'Island of Meroe', and may indicate that this was the cause of the end of Meroitic power. Two fragmentary inscriptions and a coin of Axumite origin found at Meroe suggest some kind of Axumite occupation (Plate 28a).

Whatever the truth of the end of the Meroitic state, it is clear enough that during the latter part of the fourth century AD there were considerable changes in the Nile valley. A new type of mound burial, presumed to date from the fourth and fifth centuries AD, exists in considerable numbers from south of the confluence of the Blue and White Niles to at least as far down-stream as Tanqasi, not far from the earlier centre of Napata. These burials contain distinctively different grave goods from those of earlier times – much of it is a pottery very different from that known from Meroe and other sites of Meroitic times. This pottery, not made on the wheel as were most Meroitic wares, consists of large, bulbous vessels usually, and probably rightly, known as 'beer pots'. The burials associated with these pots – no occupation sites are so far known – suggest the presence of a people different from those of Meroe, and it is tempting to see in them the people described in the Ezana inscription as the Noba. There are ambiguities in the inscription, but Ezana says that the Noba were occupying an area along the river Atbara and that they were the people against whom he fought. The implication is that they dwelled in an area already under Axumite control and that they had rebelled.

Although little is known of the nature of Axumite conquest and the role of the Noba, whose name is remarkably similar to that of the Nobatae of further north, there is nothing to suggest that Meroitic rule survived the middle of the fourth century and the coincidence of the approximately con-temporaneous end of Meroitic royal burials. The rise of Axum, and the appearance of new burial customs associated with a different material culture, suggests that Meroe came to an end in a welter of confusion and ethnic unrest.

The recent discovery at Hobagi, west of the Nile not far from Meroe, of large burial mounds with rich contents suggests the presence of important and powerful chiefs at some time after the end of the Meroitic state. More details are awaited but the evidence may be there for a re-assessment of events in the later fourth century AD.

Further north, in Nubia proper, where Meroitic settlement had increased in size and prosperity in the first few centuries AD and where many towns and villages had developed, there does not seem to have been such a violent change as may have taken place in the south. New cultural elements appear early in the fifth century AD, and though showing resemblances to Meroitic ones, they also have some marked differences. This culture – sometimes known as that of the X-Group, continuing the alphabetic system introduced by Reisner, but more often now called the Ballana culture from the most spectacular excavated site of the period – shows material much of which is a natural development from that of Meroitic times. There is a suggestion of a new people coming in, at least as chiefs, and the dramatic mound burials at Ballana and Qustul, which must be those of powerful rulers, contain a large number of luxury objects imported from Egypt and the eastern Mediterranean. These include much silver and jewellery, many bronze objects, boxes inlaid with ivory, elaborate horse trappings and weapons, and crowns closely resembling those worn by kings of Meroe as known from temple reliefs.

Though we can assume that the main agricultural population continued its life much as before, the presence of these rich burials and similar but less elaborate ones at Qasr Ibrim, Gemai and Firka suggest that some new element had entered the Nile valley. Classical writers tell us that two warlike and previously unknown groups, the Nobatae and the Blemmyes, were in the area at this time and it is reasonable to try to identify these chiefly burials with one or the other. The most commonly accepted view is that the burials are to be identified with the Nobatae, whose origins are obscure. The sixth century AD Greek writer Procopius says that they came from the western oases, and were invited to the Nile valley by the Roman emperor Diocletian (AD 285–305) to fill a gap left by his withdrawal of the Roman garrison of northern Lower Nubia and to control the Blemmyes. The Blemmyes were a people of the eastern desert, ancestors of the modern Bega, and presumably the same as the Medjay known from pharaonic times.

The close resemblance of the name of the Nobatae to that of the slightly later kingdom of Nobatia and with that of Nubia and of the Noba, suggests that the Nobatae were the introducers of Nubian language to the Nile valley, the language of the coming medieval period, which eventually replaced Meroitic as the written language of the area.

Meroitic written documents are not found after the end of the fourth century AD and such few writings as exist for the next 350 years are in Greek. The most famous of these Greek inscriptions is that of Silko, prince (Greek *basiliskos*) of the Nobatae, inscribed, in the late fifth or early sixth century AD, as a secondary inscription on a wall of the temple of Kalabsha, ancient Talmis, which was originally built in the time of the Emperor Augustus. In this inscription Silko describes a victory over the Blemmyes in the following words: 'I, Silko, prince of the Nobatae and of all the Ethiopians, came to Talmis and to Taphis. Twice I fought with the Blemmyes, and god gave me the victory.' The use of the phrase 'god gave me the victory' has suggested that Silko may have been a Christian, but the use of the word 'god' does not necessarily imply the Christian god nor does anything else about the inscription support this suggestion, including the elaborate headdress, worn by Silko, similar to ones found in the burials at Ballana.

CHAPTER 7

CHRISTIAN NUBIA AND THE COMING OF ISLAM

The two centuries or so after the collapse of the centralized Meroitic state during the fourth century AD are confusing and obscure, with various peoples – the Noba, the Nobatae, the Blemmyes – playing a little understood role in the development of the history and culture of the Nile valley. The rich graves of the Ballana period, probably of chiefs of the Nobatae, imply some centralized power and they may be those of rulers, of whom Silko, who defeated the Blemmyes in the mid-fifth century, was perhaps one. The considerable archaeological activity in Lower Nubia resulting from the Aswan dam salvage campaign of the 1960s has provided much information on the material culture of the time, though rather less on historical details. South of the second cataract we are much less well informed, though excavations at Old Dongola and at Soba, which will be described later, have provided some information.

Whatever the political situation in Lower Nubia, archaeology shows that for the majority of the population life went on much as it had always done. The introduction of the ox driven water wheel into Nubia from Egypt, perhaps in the first century BC, had led to improved agricultural methods, which in turn led to larger settlements and increased population. This increase starting in late Meroitic times, and becoming greater in subsequent centuries is clearly demonstrated by the remains that have been found. Cultural changes certainly happened, and material objects developed new styles both as a result of internal changes in fashion and, to a large extent, of influences from the north.

What also changed from the sixth century was the dominant religion, from a paganism compounded of late Egyptian ideas with Meroitic variations, to Christianity. There is also the appearance of a previously unknown language, Nubian. The two events may not be connected more than coincidentally, and since languages can only be known when found in written form there is a period after the last Meroitic inscriptions of the fourth century AD and the first Nubian ones of the eighth when we have no knowledge of the language of the country. The few extant documents are all written in Greek, which was certainly not the spoken language of the region. It may be that Nubian, to be discussed further below, had been a language of the Nile valley from much earlier times, or it may have been introduced by the Nobatae. Wherever its origins – and the existence today of related languages to the west of the Nile suggests that it was from the west – we know that it was the written and almost certainly the spoken language of much of Nubia for many centuries, and it still survives though now geographically much restricted.

The coming of Christianity made for marked changes in the political and cultural life of Nubia, changes which lasted for at least eight hundred years. Egypt had already become Christian by the end of the third century AD, and served as a base from which Christian missions could enter Nubia. The Egyptian, or Coptic, church which, during the years of Byzantine rule in Egypt had increasingly become a focus for Egyptian nationalism, broke away from the main body of orthodox Christianity after the Council of Chalcedon had declared, in AD 451, the Coptic doctrine of the single nature of Christ (monophysitism) to be heretical, but there remained adherents of the orthodox church, and these two different theological doctrines were responsible for the two missions which would enter Nubia in the sixth century.

The ending of pagan worship in the temple of Philae, at the northern limit of Nubia, by the emperor Justinian in AD 539, caused a cessation of the pilgrimage which many Nubians had been making to worship the goddess Isis, who was much revered in Meroitic and immediately post-Meroitic times, and provided an opportunity for Christian missionary activity in Nubia. It has been suggested that Christianity had already been present in Nubia on a small scale before the beginning of the main missionary effort, but evidence for this is slight. Objects bearing the symbol of the cross and other Christian emblems have been found in graves of the fifth and early sixth centuries, but these, imported from Egypt, represent the religion of their makers rather than of the users. The claim that there was a church whose ruins were found under the cathedral of Faras, and thought to date from early in the fifth century, is based on very slight evidence.

The formal introduction of Christianity and the conversion of the rulers, followed by that of much, perhaps a majority, of the population came in the middle of the sixth century, probably during the reign of a Nubian king named Eirpanome who is recorded in an inscription in Coptic in the temple at Dendur of this date. The inscription describes the turning of the pagan temple, originally built in the time of the emperor Augustus (30 BC-AD 14), into a Christian church – an event which had happened already at Philae, and was repeated in other temples throughout Nubia, as had happened in Egypt at an earlier date.

Two separate Christian missions were sent to Nubia. The first and, it seems, more successful, was a Coptic monophysite one under the patronage of the Byzantine empress Theodora in AD 543. This mission, consisting of or led by

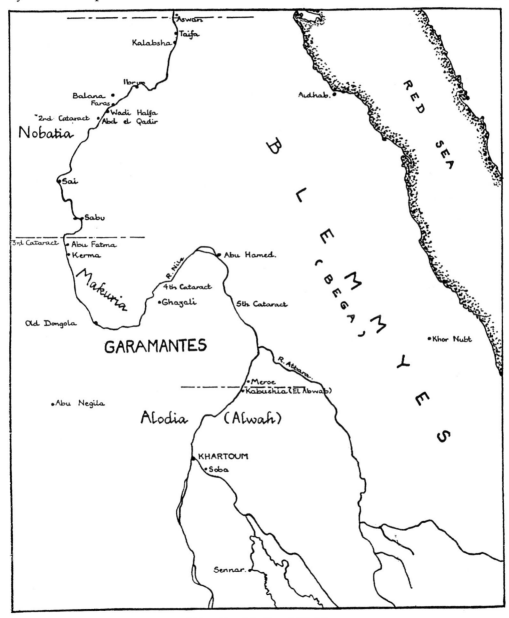

Map 10. Medieval Nubia

Julian, an associate of Theodore, the bishop of Philae, had considerable success in converting the ruler of Nobatia and many of his people. Subsequently Theodore took Julian's place in Nubia when, after two years, the latter returned to Byzantium. Theodore in turn was followed by Longinus, who arrived in Nubia in about AD 569 and stayed at the capital of the kingdom of Nobatia – almost certainly at Faras – for a few years and, in AD 580 at the invitation of the king of Alwa, the southernmost Nubian kingdom, travelled to its capital at Soba on the Blue Nile. The journey was a hazardous one, and hostility by the third Nubian state, Makuria, made it impossible for Longinus to travel by the Nile route, and he was forced to go far to the east where he was helped by the Bega to reach his destination. His mission was successful, and king and people are claimed to have been quickly converted.

The other mission, encouraged by the emperor Justinian, was from the orthodox or Melkite church and, if the partisan account is right, Makuria was converted in about AD 570. There has been much discussion of the theological allegiance of the Nubians, a matter which can have been of little concern to the majority of Nubian peasants, and the original clear-cut division of the country into orthodox and monophysite kingdoms is probably an oversimplification. Tombstones, found in large numbers and inscribed, some in Greek, some in Coptic, show that prayers of the orthodox church were widely used, though the bulk of the evidence suggests that the Nubian church was predominantly monophysite (plate 32b). Probably, as in Egypt, both sides had supporters.

What we do learn from these early missionary accounts is that Nubia was divided into three separate kingdoms. Nobatia, with its capital at Faras, stretched from the first to the third cataract, coincided neatly with the kingdom ruled earlier by Silko and his successor Aburni, and, as the name suggests, was that of the Nobatae. Makuria, extending from the third cataract perhaps to the fourth or fifth cataracts, or even to the junction of the Nile with the Atbara, cannot be easily identified with an earlier entity. It can be supposed that its capital was at Old Dongola, later to be the royal residence for a united northern Nubian kingdom, though excavations carried out at the site for the last twenty years have not as yet shown any material from the sixth century. To the south and equivalent to the southern part of the old Meroitic state was Alodia (Alwa), of which the site of Soba has been accepted as the royal residence.

The missions seem to have been remarkably successful and within a short period Christianity had become the religion of both rulers and ruled. The evidence is to be seen in the rather sudden change of burial customs from those of post-Meroitic (X-Group or Ballana) style with their abundance of grave goods, and for the chiefly burials the custom of human and animal sacrifice, to a strictly Christian one in which, with few exceptions, the body was buried without any accompanying objects. The first churches were built some time after AD 600, taking the place of re-used pagan temples. One of these, at Faras, had been, like the temple at Dendur, turned into a church by the middle of the sixth century and has been, from its presence at Faras, guessed to be the first church to be used by a ruler for the practice of the new faith.

It was just a century after the introduction of Christianity that the first contacts were made with the new conquerors of Egypt. The Arabs had over-run Egypt in the years AD 639–41 and it was not long before they turned their attention to Nubia. In AD 641 a Muslim force penetrated south of the first cataract under the leadership of 'Uqba ibn Nafi', a half-brother of Amr ibn al-'As, the conqueror of Egypt. An account of this first attack on Nubia is given by the Arabic writer Al-Baladhuri in the following words:

> When the Muslims conquered Egypt, Amr ibn al-'As sent to the vil-lages which surround it cavalry to overcome them and sent 'Uqba ibn Nafi', who was a brother of al-'As. The cavalry entered the land of Nubi like the summer campaigns against the Greeks. The Muslims found that the Nubians fought strongly, and they met showers of arrows until the majority were wounded and returned with many wounded and blinded eyes. So the Nubians were called 'pupil smiters'.

The description of the Nubians as archers is of considerable interest since archery had been identified with Nubia since Pharaonic Egyptian times, when one of the names for the people of Nubia was the 'Land of the Bow', and Nubian mercenaries are often depicted with bows in Egyptian representations. Bows and arrows have been found in Meroitic graves and the lion-headed god Apedemek is frequently represented in Meroitic art holding a bow and several arrows. This skill in archery seems to have made an impression on the Arabs and Al-Baladhuri goes on to say:

> I saw one of them [i.e. the Nubians] saying to a Muslim, 'Where would you like me to place my arrow in you', and when the Muslim replied, 'In such a place', he would not miss. . . . One day they came out against us and formed a line; we wanted to use swords, but we were not able to, and they shot at us and put out eyes to the number of one hundred and fifty.

The next major military activity was in AD 651 when a Muslim army advanced as far as Old Dongola, shortly to become the capital of a united Nubian kingdom, and by the use of catapults attacked the town and damaged the buildings. Perhaps as a result of this campaign a permanent peace treaty was made, which remained in force for several centuries. This treaty, known as the *baqt*, possibly from the Greek *pakton*, was of an unusual type and was certainly not one dictated by victors to a defeated enemy. There was some element of reciprocity about it, and in return for the delivery of slaves by the Nubians the Muslims provided food supplies, wine and cloth. This unusual type of treaty may have been the renewal of a longstanding arrangement going back to Roman times, continued and endorsed again by the new rulers of Egypt.

Whatever the intention of the makers of the treaty, it was of importance for Nubia, since it resulted in about five hundred years of peaceful relations with their northern and more powerful neighbours, and allowed the development of a distinctive Nubian culture under predominantly peaceful conditions. During the years following the making of the treaty a native Nubian culture developed, of which the main aspects known to us are the ruins of churches (Plates 29b, 31a) and the development of a very distinctive and attractive ceramic art. The culture of the literate Nubian civilization had a distinct Byzantine and Coptic flavour, particularly in the church decoration, best known from the paintings in the cathedral at Faras.

Politically the most important event was the combining of the two states of Nobatia and Makuria into one. The exact date at which this happened is not known but it must have been in the latter part of the seventh or early eighth centuries, perhaps between AD 690 and 710. In the latter year a king of Nubia, Merkurios, put up an inscription at Taifa. So it is assumed that by this date Makuria had either absorbed Nobatia or that there had been an agreement between the two to amalgamate. Culture and language were identical in the two parts of the new kingdom and amalgamation cannot have meant much of a change, even though the capital was now established at Old Dongola, formerly the capital of Makuria only. Nobatia maintained some aspects of its separate identity and the eparch of Nobatia, a governor whose horned head-dress and other distinctive emblems are known from several church paintings, continued to be an official of importance.

An Egyptian Christian writer, John the Deacon, writing in c.AD 768 described King Merkurios as the 'New Constantine', suggesting that he played some important role in Nubian Christianity, and it may be that it was in his reign that the monophysites became the dominant force in the Nubian church. If this was so we are faced with the curious situation that, if the theological allegiances of the two kingdoms were as have been suggested, the one that was incorporated into the new unified kingdom of Dongola imposed its views onto the one that became dominant. This seems unlikely, and is probably a reflection of the fact that we do not fully understand the rather fluid theological allegiances of the time.

The beginning of the reign of Merkurios can now be fixed with certainty since the finding at Faras of a foundation stone dated in the year AD 707 which states that it was placed in position in his eleventh year. This puts his accession in AD 697 and, since the same inscription gives the name of the fifth bishop of Faras, Paulos, implies that the see was founded early in the seventh century. The story of the fusion of the two states is far from clear and it is noticeable that the Arab accounts of the invasion of the mid-seventh century only speak of one kingdom and state that the capital was at Dongola which was the target of the invaders. This may mean that a separate Nobatia had disappeared earlier than is generally supposed.

From the early eighth century there is much material for the study of the political and cultural development of Christian Nubia. There is historical information from Arab writers and archaeological excavations have contributed much to our understanding of the life and culture of the time. During the next few centuries Nubia was at the height of its prosperity and political importance and many towns and villages flourished along the banks of the Nile, taking advantage of a stable and regular Nile flood which provided the opportunity for agricultural development (Plate 31b). Settlements grew larger and some, such as Debeira, Ermenna and Mainarti grew to be sizeable towns. Domestic architecture developed and the characteristic Nubian brick vault became the normal method of roofing. It can still be seen today in the villages of the northernmost Nubians who were moved to the region of Kom Ombo by the Egyptian government when Lake Nubia began to fill. The very obvious population increase is demonstrated by the presence of many towns and villages, nearly all with associated churches, from south of Aswan to the fourth cataract. The style of building and the very distinctive painted pottery (Plate 30) which was introduced by the middle of the eighth century makes the identification of settlements of the period an easy matter. There was Christian settlement even up stream of the fourth cataract, and villages and churches with tombstones have been found in the region of the fifth cataract, which seems to be the southern limit of the culture known in northern Nubia. Further up stream there is material of a different sort from the kingdom whose capital at Soba has been recently excavated with dramatic results. Small amounts of pottery of well known northern Nubian types have been found there together with imported Islamic ceramics and glass which show that the town was flourishing at the same time as the kingdom of Dongola, and in contact through trading activities with the wider Islamic world.

During this period Nubia was a military power of some significance and there is a story that a Nubian army entered Egypt and captured the Egyptian capital at Fostat. This is probably a fabricated story, but parts of Upper Egypt were in Nubian occupation on several occasions and in AD 862 the Nubians went as far as Akhmim and for a time Edfu was a centre of Nubian culture. Military activity was also carried out against the Bega of the Red Sea hills and to attempt to stem Arab infiltration in the gold mining areas located there. The Arabs had penetrated the area sufficiently to have built a mosque at Sinkat and treaties were made in the ninth century defining the rights of Muslims. The existence of a number of tombstones written in Arabic with Muslim funerary formulae at various places in Nubia, at Mainarti and Debeira East and inscriptions in Arabic on the walls of buildings in the Christian town at Debeira West are evidence for Arab penetration. At Khor Nubt in the Red Sea hills a group of Arabic tombstones dates from shortly after the middle of the ninth century AD.

Although Arab writers suggest considerable military power by the Nubians, archaeology does not confirm this, and from the large number of sites that have been excavated there are no traces of military weapons. If we were dependent only on archaeological evidence Nubian society would have to be described as a peaceful agricultural one, deeply religious, as shown by the large number of churches and by the presence of Christian symbols on many of the artifacts. The peaceful conditions which prevailed in most of Nubia are shown by the open and unfortified nature of most of the towns and villages, but in the northerly area closer to Egypt there are several fortified towns. Ikhmindi had been the site of a fort since the sixth century AD, as a foundation inscription of a king Tokiltoeton demonstrates. Tokiltoeton was perhaps the successor of Eirpanome, already mentioned as the first king to be converted to Christianity. Ikhmindi remained a strongly fortified town throughout medieval times.

Medieval Nubia was a literate society, and documents written in the old Nubian language first appear in the eighth century AD. The earliest dated example of written Old Nubian is from a graffito in the temple of Ramesses II, subsequently used as a church at Wadi el Sebua. This graffito, containing a prayer, is dated using the Era of the Martyrs, a dating system commonly used in medieval Nubia, which begins in the year AD 284, a time of widespread persecution of Christians in Egypt by the Roman emperor Diocletian. From the eighth century on a number of documents are known and the number substantially increased with the finding of many writings at Qasr Ibrim. The language of the documents, Old Nubian, is ancestral to the Mahas dialect of Nubian still spoken today along a stretch of the Nile between Wadi Halfa and the third cataract. The writing system is the Coptic form of the Greek alphabet with the addition of three signs, probably borrowed from Meroitic, to represent sounds in Old Nubian which do not exist in Coptic.

The documents as known at present are mostly religious in nature and content but there are some dealing with lay matters such as land tenure and the disposal of slaves. The recently published Qasr Ibrim texts add considerably to the body of lay documents. The documents are of especial interest from a linguistic and cultural standpoint; they are, as yet, of little historical value, although a leather document found at Gebel Adda tells of a previously unknown king, and gives evidence for a small local kingdom.

Figure 30. Nubian writing

Writing was widespread in Nubia, although literacy may have been restricted to a small group, and was used not only for formal documents but also for many graffiti. Many tombstones have been found and it is noticeable that Old Nubian was scarcely ever used for this purpose. It was however used for liturgical purposes and the three languages, Old Nubian, Greek and Coptic, were all in use, though it can be assumed that Old Nubian was the vernacular.

The reading and understanding of the Old Nubian documents has been much facilitated by the presence of an existing spoken language, as also by their being written with a known writing system, and important advances in the knowledge of the language have been made in recent years much helped by the finding of many new documents. Understanding has been much helped by many Old Nubian texts being translations from known Greek religious ones.

The best known and most spectacular evidence for the high standard of Nubian culture is to be seen in its church architecture and in the many paintings with which these churches were decorated. Of the ecclesiastical

127

buildings the best preserved was the cathedral at Faras excavated by a Polish expedition from 1961 to 1964. At this place, under what at first appeared to be a large sand dune, a cathedral was found, whose walls were covered with paintings, well preserved by the fortunate filling of the building with sand, after the roof had collapsed. This cathedral had originally been built in the seventh century on the site of an earlier building, at a town which had been an important administrative centre in Meroitic times, and continued to be so for many centuries. The seventh-century building was renewed in AD 707, and two foundation stones, one in Greek, one in Coptic, were set up by Paulos the fifth bishop of Faras. Both stones mention King Merkurios, presumably the same as the 'New Constantine', already referred to as the possible unifier of Nobatia and Makuria. This rebuilding considerably enlarged the earlier structure, and the cathedral then consisted of a nave and four aisles. A magnificent series of frescoes covered the walls, the first being painted in about AD 750. Painting on the cathedral walls continued at least until the eleventh century, and detailed study has made it possible to date the various artistic styles and the use of different colours. Most of the paintings are of religious themes. There is a splendid one of the nativity and there are also depictions of saints, bishops and a few royalties including one showing 'Martha the queen mother' being protected by the Virgin Mary who holds the child Jesus in her arms. This painting, probably from the end of the eleventh century, is of particular interest since it shows the importance which the mother of the king had in the Nubian kingdom. It gives a fine example of Nubian royal robes and, by showing the face of the queen in darker tones than that of the Virgin, indicates that the Nubian artist was intending to show that it was a representation of one of his own people, and it may be a portrait. All those depicted in the paintings who might be supposed to be Nubians, kings and bishops, are shown darker than Christ, saints, and other holy personages.

The cathedral and surrounding buildings have also produced much other historical information. Foundation stones of several kings are known, some providing dates. Several eparchs of Nubia are depicted and, the most valuable of all, there is a list of bishops painted on a wall in a chapel, which gives their names and lengths of reign and, in some cases, the month and day (but not the year) of death. Since tombstones with the year of death have been found for some of these bishops, it has been possible to reconstruct the chronology of part of the list, though damage prevents a complete restoration.

The paintings have provided an enormous amount of information, not only for the painting styles of Nubia and their variation at different times, but have also given details of ecclesiastical practice, of iconography, and of ecclesiastical and royal dress.

At some time early in the tenth century there was a fire in the cathedral which caused considerable damage particularly to the roof, which was then rebuilt in a different style, and the original wooden one was replaced by the typical Nubian brick barrel vault. The granite columns of the nave were replaced by brick piers, and the main west door was bricked up. During the period, when the building was out of use during rebuilding, a new church was built to the south, and a foundation stone with the date AD 930 is good evidence for the date of the re-modelling of the cathedral. The final damage was in about AD 1170 when the central dome and the nave vault collapsed, or perhaps were destroyed. The roof of the nave was never rebuilt and it was this lucky chance that caused the cathedral to fill with wind-blown sand, thus preserving the frescoes. In many other churches where the paintings have been left exposed to the ravages of time and damage by those of another faith, they have often been destroyed beyond hope of restoration.

During these centuries various details of the history of the area are known, particularly concerning relations with Muslim Egypt. There is an account of a visit to Baghdad by George the son of King Zakaria in the year AD 836, to explain to the Abbasid caliph Mu'tasim why the *baqt* payments had not been kept up. Another version of the story suggests that George went only as far as Cairo and that a new treaty was made reducing the *baqt* payment from every year to every three years.

During the ninth century the Arabs penetrated the valuable gold-producing areas of the Red Sea hills and an independent Arab leader, al-'Omari, tried to establish his rights there. He also raided the Nile valley and carried out sporadic warfare against the Nubians. We have some details of events of the time and the names of Nubian kings, of whom George I (c.AD 860–920) is the best known – his portrait is known from Faras where his appearance lends verisimilitude to the long reign with which he is credited. His nephew Niuty was charged with leading an army against al-'Omari but later rebelled against his uncle, and there followed years of intrigue and counter-intrigue, a situation which was to become even more common in Nubia in later times. Niuty was ultimately killed, George's son Zakaria continued to be embroiled with the Arabs, and sporadic warfare continued until the middle of the tenth century.

With the coming to power in Egypt of the Fatimids in AD 969 two centuries of comparative peace began and Nubia continued to be prosperous. Our information comes almost exclusively from Arab writers who give such details as the erection of a red brick building at Old Dongola by King Raphael in AD 1002. The recent excavations have found many churches, but have not identified King Raphael's building. A King Solomon (died AD 1081) is recorded as having been buried in the monastery of St George at Khandaq, a building which has not been identified, though there are many Christian remains to be seen at this town.

The names of several of the kings are known from this time, but we do not know for certain how the claim to the throne was established, though there is some evidence to suggest that succession was from a ruler to his sister's son and this may be the reason for the importance given to the 'king's mother' in two paintings at Faras. Royal vestments are known from the Faras paintings and the royal regalia consisted of a throne, a parasol, a crown and a gold bracelet; although this sounds very splendid, and the frescoes certainly suggest this, when the ambassador of Turan Shah of Egypt came to Dongola in about AD 1175 he described the king as riding out to meet him in very simple dress, and on a horse without any elaborate trappings.

Details of the nature of the administration are few, but we have the titles of a number of court officials, several of them derived from Byzantine ones. The eparch of Nubia was the most important of the functionaries of the kingdom. He resided at Faras and continued to rule what was once the independent kingdom of Nobatia and the earlier Meroitic province. His function is not known in detail, but not only did he control the northernmost part of the kingdom but he was also in charge of dealings with Egypt and with foreign merchants and travellers – he had the additional title of 'Lord of the Mountain' or perhaps 'Lord of the Horses' (the Arabic version of his title has been read both ways). He wore a distinctive garment and regalia of which the main element was a two-horned head-dress. At first based at Faras, the traditional capital of the northern province, he later moved his residence to Qasr Ibrim which, safe on its hill top, was much easier to defend.

The coming to power in Egypt of the Ayyubid ruler Salah el-Din, and the end of the Fatimid dynasty, resulted in further attacks on Nubia and in AD 1173 Turan Shah, a brother of Salah el-Din, attacked Nubia and captured the strong point of Qasr Ibrim, where he took many prisoners, turned the church into a mosque, and slaughtered the large number of pigs which the Christian inhabitants had kept. The fort and town were thoroughly pillaged and reference is made particularly to the removal of large stocks of cotton. A Muslim garrison was placed there under the command of Ibrahim el Kurdi, but a few years later Ibrahim was drowned at Adendan, not far from Faras. Shortly after this the garrison of Qasr Ibrim was withdrawn, and the Christians returned and restored the church. The Nubians were now left undisturbed for about one hundred years, perhaps as a result of an unfavourable report on the economic potential of the country, made by a Muslim mission which was sent to Dongola.

The main evidence for the nature of domestic and economic life during the period which ended with the seizure of power in Egypt by the Mamluks (AD 1250) is provided by archaeology, and a great many towns, villages and other settlements have been investigated during the last twenty-five years. There is now much information on the architecture of both churches and private dwellings and it is clear that Nubia was more thickly populated at this time than at any other period. Most of the settlements are small villages, nearly always accompanied by a church, but there are also a few fortified settlements such as Ikhmindi, already referred to, Sabagura and a few others. Towns are known from Gebel Adda, Faras (of especial importance as the residence of the Eparch), Qasr Ibrim with its unique position on top of a large hill, the interesting island site of Mainarti, Debeira West and a number of others.

The heavily ecclesiastical character of Nubian remains is strengthened by the existence of two monasteries, at Wizz, very close to Faras, and at Ghazali, but it may be that there were others either not found or not identified as monasteries, like one of the building complexes at Debeira West, which the excavator suggested was a monastery though this could not be confirmed. It is possible that the monasteries were largely inhabited by Coptic monks escaping from persecution in Egypt especially at the time of the Caliph el-Hakim el Mansur (AD 996–1021) in whose time there was considerable persecution of the Coptic population of Egypt. The evidence from the grave-stones found at Ghazali certainly suggest that the majority of the monks were

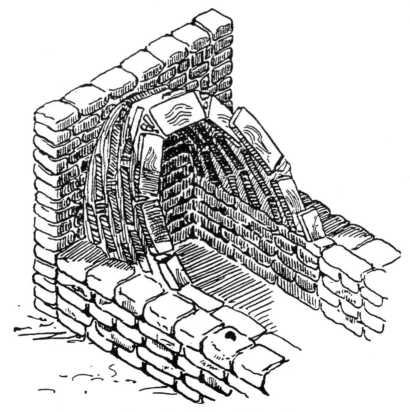

Figure 31. Nubian brick vault
(*after* G. S. Mileham, *Churches in Lower Nubia*, Philadelphia, 1910)

131

Copts since of 79 inscribed grave stones found there 47 were in Coptic and only 19 in Greek. The remainder were too fragmentary for the language to be determined. It was also very noticeable that whereas those written in Coptic were accurately and grammatically written those in Greek were often faulty.

The main building material for all the structures was mud brick, the traditional and appropriate building material of the country. Only in a few cases was stone used, and then mainly for ecclesiastical buildings of importance. The domestic dwellings were generally close-packed small houses usually roofed with the distinctive Nubian arch, and were markedly different from most of the villages of Nubia today where flat-roofed houses stand separated by open spaces and strung out along the bank of the river. At some time in the history of Nubia there must have been a very noticeable change in architectural style except, strangely enough, in the most northerly part, where one would have expected Egyptian influence to have been strongest. Today the traditional vault, as known from many ancient villages, is only to be found in the area around Aswan inhabited by the Kenuz branch of the Nubian people.

Ecclesiastical architecture is well known from the large number of churches, and the way in which the style and lay-out changed through the centuries has been studied by Adams, and modified somewhat by other scholars. Starting with very small plain buildings of which the oldest may go back to the sixth century, the churches became larger and, strongly influenced by the styles of the eastern Christian church, developed along very much the same lines as did churches in Egypt. There were some special and distinctive elements in Nubian church design, especially the presence of a passage running behind the apse-shaped sanctuary, a feature which is not known in other contemporary Christian churches of the Near East.

Of objects found in Nubian settlements, by far the most numerous are the ceramics. In Christian times Nubian ceramic art reached its high point, and a great variety of styles, both plain and painted, were produced in enormous number. The best known are the various painted styles, dating from c.AD 850 to c.AD 1100, which show a great range of decoration both figurative and geometric. The different pottery types have been studied in detail and a firm chronology has been developed which makes it possible to date remains of the Christian period with reasonable accuracy (Plate 30).

The last few hundred years of Christian Nubia show a steady decline in material prosperity and in artistic production, and this appears to be linked with increasing political confusion. The Mamluk rulers of Egypt were notably more aggressive than their Ayyubid predecessors and took advantage of what appear to have been a series of dynastic feuds in the Nubian royal family based at Dongola. In 1275 there occurred what may have been the first of several attempts to use Egyptian help to solve dynastic quarrels in Nubia, when Shekanda went to Egypt to request support in a claim against the reigning king David. Sultan Beybars of Egypt supported Shekanda and sent a force into Nubia which put him on the throne, but then enforced further payments of tribute and exerted some direct control over the northern part of Nubia. The last Christian king that we know to have ruled from Dongola was Kudanbes, who came to the throne in about AD 1310. By this time Muslim influence was becoming increasingly important, and in the year AD 1317 an inscription in the building at Old Dongola usually thought of as a palace, says that it was turned into a mosque. It seems certain that part, at least, of the Nubian population had now become Muslim and certainly the Banu Kanz, ancestors of the modern Kenuz Nubians of the Aswan area, had done so.

By the fourteenth century the situation had become increasingly chaotic. We know that the small Nubian kingdom of Do-tawo was established at Gebel Adda, perhaps after the destruction of Old Dongola, and documents from Gebel Adda show that it persisted into the fifteenth century, one document being dated to AD 1484 and giving the name of a king, Joel, and of a bishop. We know that Qasr Ibrim had remained the seat of a bishopric into at least the late fourteenth century, since the burial of bishop Timotheos who was consecrated in 1372 was found there. It is also of interest that Timotheos was consecrated in Cairo at the well known church of el Moallaqa in Old Cairo, showing that the Nubian church took its authority from Egypt, and was probably subordinate to the Coptic patriarch. Muslim and Arab pressure was increasing throughout this period, and it seems that there was a gradual conversion of the population to the new religion. In the northern part of Nubia, where incoming Arabs would not have found the land especially attractive, they did not settle in large numbers, and probably for this reason the Nubian language has persisted to this day.

Further south was the southern Nubian kingdom of Alwa whose centre at Soba was a short way up the Blue Nile from its juncture with the White Nile. Soba was a large town with several ecclesiastical and administrative buildings. It was described by Arab writers, and the recent excavations have provided much additional information. Details of its history are not well known, though the name of a king David who died in AD 1015 has been obtained from a recently found tombstone. Apart from this Soba remained in comparative obscurity until its end.

The good grazing of this central Sudan kingdom made it more attractive to Arab groups than the desert and river-side cultivation of further north. It seems that, from at least the fourteenth century, groups of Arabs moved into the area and formed a unified tribe, the Abdullab who, with their capital of Qerri close to the sixth cataract, became formidable opponents of the kingdom of Soba.

133

The usually accepted story is that Soba was captured in AD 1504 by Umara Dunqas, the leader of the Fung, a people from the upper part of the Blue Nile who had established their capital at Sennar. The Abdullab are said to have allied themselves with the Fung to bring about the end of Soba. An alternative view is that the Abdullab had already conquered Soba, perhaps as early as the fourteenth century AD, and that the Fung in their turn achieved rule over the Abdullab. Whatever the precise details, the Christian traditions of Soba came to an end, and the Arabic language and the Islamic religion were completely accepted in a very short time.

BIBLIOGRAPHY

Abbas Sid Ahmed. 'The Antiquities of Mograt Island.' *Sudan Notes and Records* XLII (1971): 1–22.

Abbas Mohammed Ali and A.E. Marks. 'The Prehistory of Shaqadud in the Western Butana, Central Sudan: A Preliminary Report.' *Norwegian Archaeological Review* 17 (1984): 52–9.

Adams, William Y. 'Architectural Evolution of the Nubian Church, 500–1400 A.D.' *Journal of the American Research Center in Egypt* IV (1965): 87–139.

Adams, William Y. *Meroitica North and South. Meroitica* 2. Berlin, 1976.

Adams, William Y. *Nubia, Corridor to Africa*. London, 1977.

Adams, William Y. 'Doubts about the "Lost Pharaohs."' *Journal of Near Eastern Studies* 44 (1985), 185–92.

Adams, William Y. *Ceramic Industries of Mediaeval Nubia*. 2 volumes. Lexington. 1986.

Addison, F. *Jebel Moya*. 2 volumes. Oxford, 1949.

Ahmed, Khidir Abdelkarim. *Meroitic Settlement in the Central Sudan*. Cambridge Monographs in African Archaeology 8. BAR International Series 197. Oxford 1984.

Arkell, A.J. *The Old Stone Age in the Anglo-Egyptian Sudan*. Sudan Antiquities Service Occasional Papers 1. Khartoum, 1949.

Arkell, A.J. *Early Khartoum*. London, 1949.

Arkell, A.J. 'Varia Sudanica.' *Journal of Egyptian Archaeology* 36 (1950): 24–40.

Arkell, A.J. *Shaheinab*. London, 1953.

Arkell, A.J. 'Four Occupation Sites at Agordat.' *Kush* 2 (1954): 33–62.

Arkell, A.J. *A History of the Sudan to 1821*. 2nd edition. London, 1961.

Arkell, A.J. and P. Ucko. 'Review of Predynastic Development in the Nile Valley.' *Current Anthropology* 6 (1965), 145–66.

Bietak, Manfred. 'The C-Group and the Pan-Grave Culture in Nubia.' *Nubian Culture Past and Present*, ed. T. Hägg. Stockholm, 1987, 114–28.

Bietak, Manfred and R. Engelmayer. 'Eine frühdynastische Abri-Siedlung mit

Felsbildern aus Sayala – Nubien.' *Österreichische Akademie der Wissenschaften, Philosophisch-Historische Klasse* 82 (1963).

Bonnet, Charles. *Kerma, royaume de Nubie*. Geneva, 1990.

Browne, G.M. *Old Nubian Texts from Qasr Ibrim* II. London, 1989.

Browne, G.M. *Old Nubian Texts from Qasr Ibrim* III. London, 1991.

Caneva, I. et al. 'Pottery Using Gatherers and Hunters at Saggai.' *Origini Preistoria e Protostoria delle Civiltà antiche* XII (1983): 7–278.

Caneva, I. et al. *El Geili – The History of a Middle Nile Environment 7000 B.C.-A.D. 1500*. Cambridge Monographs in African Archaeology 29. BAR International Series 424. Oxford, 1988.

Clark, J. Desmond. 'Shabona: an Early Khartoum Settlement on the White Nile.' *Late Prehistory of the Nile Basin and the Sahara*, ed. L. Krzyzaniak and M. Kobusiewiz. Poznan, 1989, 387–410.

Davies, N. de G. and A.H. Gardiner. *The Tomb of Huy, Viceroy of Nubia in the Reign of Tut'ankhamun*. Theban Tomb Series, Fourth Memoir. London, 1926.

Dunham, D. *The Royal Cemeteries of Kush: I Kurru*. Boston, 1950.

Dunham, D. *The Royal Cemeteries of Kush: II Nuri*. Boston, 1955.

Dunham, D. *The Royal Cemeteries of Kush: IV Royal Tombs at Meroe and Barkal*. Boston, 1957.

Dunham, D. *The Royal Cemeteries of Kush: V The West and South Cemeteries at Meroe*. Boston, 1963.

Dunham, D. *Second Cataract Forts. Volume 2, Uronarti, Shalfak, Mirgissa*. Boston, 1967.

Dunham, D. *The Barkal Temples*. Boston, 1970.

Dunham, D. and J.M.A. Janssen. *Second Cataract Forts. Volume I, Semna, Kumma*. Boston, 1969.

Dunham, D. and M.F.L. MacAdam. 'The Names and Relationships of the Royal Family of Napata.' *Journal of Egyptian Archaeology* 35 (1949), 139–49.

Emery, W.B. *Egypt in Nubia*. London, 1965.

Emery, W.B., H.S. Smith and A. Millard. *The Fortress of Buhen: the Archaeological Report*. London, 1979.

Fairman, H.W. 'Preliminary report on the excavations at Sesibi (Sudla) and Amarah West, 1937–1938.' *Journal of Egyptian Archaeology* 24 (1938): 151–6.

Fairman, H.W. 'Preliminary report on the excavations at Amarah West 1938–1939.' *Journal of Egyptian Archaeology* 25 (1939): 139–44.

Gamer-Wallert I. and K. Zibelius. *Der Löwentempel von Naq'a in der Butana (Sudan) I*. Wiesbaden, 1983.

Gamer-Wallert, I. *Der Löwentempel von Naq'a in der Butana (Sudan) III*. Wiesbaden, 1983.

Giorgini, M.S. *Soleb I*. Florence, 1965.

Giorgini, M.S. *Soleb II*. Florence, 1971.

Gratien, Brigitte. *Les Cultures Kerma*. Lille, 1978.

Gratien, Brigitte. *Sai I – La Nécropole Kerma*. Paris, 1986.

Griffith, F.Ll. 'Oxford Excavations in Nubia.' *Liverpool Annals of Archaeology and Anthropology* IX (1922), 67–124.

Griffith, F.Ll. 'Oxford Excavations in Nubia.' *Liverpool Annals of Archaeology and Anthropology* X (1923): 73–171.

Griffith, F.Ll. 'Oxford Excavations in Nubia.' *Liverpool Annals of Archaeology and Anthropology* XI (1924): 115–25; 141–80.

Griffith, F.Ll. 'Oxford Excavations in Nubia.' *Liverpool Annals of Archaeology and Anthropology* XII (1925): 57–172.

Griffith, F.Ll. 'Oxford Excavations in Nubia.' *Liverpool Annals of Archaeology and Anthropology* XIII (1926): 17–37.

Habachi, Labib. 'The Second Stela of Kamose.' *Abhandlungen des Deutschen Archäologischen Instituts Abteilung Kairo. Ägyptologische Reihe* 8. Glückstadt, 1973.

Hakim, Ahmed Ali. 'The City of Meroe and the Myth of Napata.' *Adab* 2 and 3 (1975): 120–34.

Hasan, Yusuf Fadl. *The Arabs and the Sudan. Reprint.* Khartoum, 1973.

Hassan, Fekri. 'Prehistoric Settlements along the Main Nile.' *The Sahara and the Nile*, eds M.A.J. Williams and H. Faure. Rotterdam, 1980, 421–50.

Hassan, Fekri. 'Chronology of the Khartoum "Mesolithic" and "Neolithic" and related sites in the Sudan: statistical analysis and comparisons with Egypt.' *African Archaeological Review* 4 (1986): 83–102.

Hellström, P. and H. Langballe. *The Rock Drawings.* The Scandinavian Joint Expedition to Sudanese Nubia. Volume 1. Stockholm, 1970.

Hintze, F. 'Preliminary Report of the Butana Expedition 1958.' *Kush* VII (1959), 171–96.

Hintze, F. *Die Inschriften des Löwentempels.* Berlin, 1962.

Hintze, F. 'Das Kerma Problem.' *Zeitschrift für Ägyptische Sprache* 91 (1964): 79–86.

Hintze, F. 'Preliminary Note on the Epigraphic Expedition to Sudanese Nubia, 1963.' *Kush* XII (1964): 40–2.

Hintze, F. 'Preliminary Note on the Epigraphic Expedition to Sudanese Nubia, 1963.' *Kush* XIII (1964): 13–16.

Hintze, F. *Musawwarat es Sufra.* Vol. I, 2 *Der Löwentempel.* Tafelband. Berlin, 1971.

Hintze, Ursula. 'The Graffiti from the Great Enclosure at Musawwarat es Sufra.' *Africa in Antiquity* Meroitica 5 (1979): 135–50.

Jackson, H.C. 'A Trek in Abu Hamed District.' *Sudan Notes and Records* IX, No. 2 (1926): 1–35.

Jakobielski, S. *Faras III – A History of the Bishopric of Pachoras on the Basis of Coptic Inscriptions.* Warsaw, 1972.

Kitchen, K.A. 'Punt and How to Get There.' *Orientalia* 49 (1971): 184–207.

Kitchen, K.A. *The Third Intermediate Period in Egypt.* Warminster, 1973.

Krause, Th. 'Der Kiosk von Naqa.' *Archäologische Anzeiger* (1964): 834–68.

Krzyzaniak, L. 'The Neolithic habitation at Kadero (Central Sudan).' *Origin and Early Development of Food-Producing Cultures in North Eastern Africa*, ed. L. Krzyzaniak and M. Kobusiewicz. Poznan, 1984, 309–16.

Krzyzaniak, L. 'Early farming in the Middle Nile Basin: recent discoveries at Kadero (Central Sudan).' *Antiquity* 65 (1991), 515–32.

Lal, B.B. 'Indian Archaeological Expedition to Nubia, 1962. A Preliminary Report.' *Fouilles en Nubie (1961–1963)* (1967): 97–118.

Leclant, J. 'Kashta, Pharaon, en Egypte.' *Zeitschrift für Ägyptische Sprache und Altertumskunde* 90 (1963): 74–81.

Lenoble, P. 'A New Type of Mound Grave: Le Tumulus Enceinte d'Umm Makharoqa, près d'el Hobagi.' *Archéologie du Nil Moyen* 3 (1989), 93–120.

Macadam, M.F.L. *The Temples of Kawa*. I, II. Oxford, 1949.

Magid, A. *Plant Domestication in the Middle Nile Basin*. Cambridge Monographs in African Archaeology 35. BAR International Series 523. Oxford, 1989.

Marks, A.E. et al. 'The Prehistory of the Central Nile Valley as seen from its eastern hinterland: Excavations at Shaqadud, Sudan.' *Journal of Field Archaeology* 12 (1985): 261–78.

Michalowski, K. *Faras – Die Kathedrale aus dem Wüstensand*. Zurich, 1967.

Mohammed-Ali, Abbas S. 'Sorourab I: a Neolithic Site in Khartoum Province, Sudan.' *Current Anthropology* 25 (1984): 117–19.

Nordström, Hans Ake. *Neolithic and A-Group Sites*. Scandinavian Joint Expedition to Sudanese Nubia. Volume 3:1. Stockholm, 1972.

O'Connor, D. 'The Locations of Yam and Kush and their Historical Implications.' *Journal of the American Research Center in Egypt* XXIII (1986), 27–50.

O'Connor, D. 'The Location of Irem.' *Journal of Egyptian Archaeology* 73 (1987): 99–136.

Peters, Joris. 'A revision of the faunal remains from two Central Sudanese sites: Khartoum Hospital and Esh Shaheinab.' *Archaeozoologia. Mélanges* (1986): 11–33.

Petrie, W.M. Flinders. *Diospolis Parva: The Cemeteries of Abadiyeh and Hu 1898–1899*. London, 1901.

Piotrovsky, B.B. 'The Early Dynasty Settlement of Khor-Daoud and Wadi-Allaki, the Ancient Route of the Gold Mines.' *Fouilles en Nubie (1961–1963)* Cairo, 1967: 127–40.

Plumley, J. *The Scroll of Bishop Timotheos*. London, 1975.

Plumley, J. and G.M. Browne. *Old Nubian Texts from Qasr Ibrim* I. London, 1988.

Randall-MacIver, D. and C.L. Woolley. *Areika*. Philadelphia, 1909.

Randall-MacIver, D. and C.L. Woolley. *Buhen*. 2 volumes. Philadelphia, 1911.

Reisner, G.A. *The Archaeological Survey of Nubia, Reports for 1907–1908*. 2 volumes. Cairo, 1910.

Reisner, G.A. 'Kerma and the Viceroys of Nubia.' *Journal of Egyptian Archaeology* 6 (1920: 28–55; 73–88.

Reisner, G.A. *Excavations at Kerma*. Cambridge, Mass. 1923.

Ryder, M.L. 'Skin, Hair and Cloth Remains from the Ancient Kerma Civilization of Northern Sudan.' *Journal of Archaeological Science* 11 (1984): 477–82.

Sauneron, Serge. 'Un village nubien fortifié sur la rive orientale de Ouadi es-Sébou'.' *Bulletin de l'Institut français d'archéologie orientale* 63 (1965): 161–7.

Säve-Söderbergh, T. *Ägypten und Nubien*. Lund, 1941.

Säve-Söderbergh, T. 'Preliminary Report of the Scandinavian Joint Expedition, 1961–1962.' *Kush* XI (1963): 47–69.

Shinnie, P.L. 'Preliminary Report on the Excavations at 'Amarah West 1948–49 and 1949–50.' *Journal of Egyptian Archaeology* 37 (1951): 5–11.

Shinnie, P.L. *Meroe: A Civilization of the Sudan*. London, 1967.

Shinnie, P.L. 'The Nilotic Sudan and Ethiopia c. 660 B.C. to c. A.D. 600.' in *Cambridge History of Africa 2*, ed. J. Fage. Cambridge (1978), 210–71.

Shinnie, P.L. 'Christian Nubia.' *Cambridge History of Africa 2*. ed. J. Fage. Cambridge (1978), 556–88.

Shinnie, P.L. 'The main lines of socio-economic development in the Sudan in Post-Neolithic times.' *Origin and Early Development of Fodd-Producing Cultures in North-Eastern Africa*, ed. L. Krzyzaniak and M. Kobusiewicz. Poznan (1984), 109–15.

Shinnie, P.L. 'The Culture of Meroe and its Influence in the Central Sudan.' *Sahara* 2 (1989): 21–30.

Smith, H.S. *Preliminary Reports of the Egypt Exploration Society's Nubian Survey*. Cairo, 1962.

Smith, H.S. 'The Nubian B-Group.' *Kush* 14 (1966): 69–124.

Steindorff, Georg. *Aniba*. Volumes 1 and 2. Glückstadt, 1935, 1937.

Török, L. *Late Antique Nubia*. Budapest, 1988.

Trigger, B.G. *History and Settlement in Lower Nubia*. Yale University Publications in Anthropology No. 69. New Haven, 1965.

Trigger, B.G. *Nubia under the Pharaohs*. London, 1976.

Vantini, G. *Oriental Sources Concerning Nubia*. Heidelberg and Warsaw, 1975.

Vercoutter, J. 'New Egyptian Texts from the Sudan.' *Kush* (1956), 66–82.

Vercoutter, J. 'Un Palais des "Candaces" Contemporain d'Auguste.' *Syria* XXXIX (1962), 263–99.

Vercoutter, J. *Mirgissa*, I, II, III. Paris 1970, 1975, 1976.

Vila, A. 'L'Armement de la Forteresse de Mirgissa – Iken.' *Révue d' Egyptologie* 22 (1970): 171–99.

Vila, A. *La prospection archéologique de la vallée du Nil, au sud de la cataracte de Dal*. Fasc. 12 (1980); 13 (1982); 14 (1984); 15 (1985). Paris.

Villard, U. Monneret de. *Storia della Nubia Cristiana*. Rome, 1938.

Welsby, D.A. and C.M. Daniels. *Soba – Archaeological Research at a Medieval Capital on the Blue Nile*. Memoirs of the British Institute in Eastern Africa, 12. London, 1991.

Wendorf, F. *The Prehistory of Nubia*. 2 volumes. Fort Burgwin, 1968.

Wendorf, F., R. Schild and H. Haas. 'New Radiocarbon Chronology for Prehistoric Sites in Nubia.' *Journal of Field Archaeology* 6 (1979): 219–33.

Wenzel, Marian. *House Decoration in Nubia*. London, 1972.

Whiteman, A.J. *The Geology of the Sudan Republic*. Oxford, 1971.

Williams, Bruce. 'The Lost Pharaohs of Nubia.' *Archaeology* 33 no. 5 (1980): 12–21.

Williams, Bruce. 'Forebears of Menes in Nubia: Myth or Reality?' *Journal of Near Eastern Studies* 46 (1987): 15–26.

Williams, Bruce. *University of Chicago Oriental Institute Nubian Expedition, Vol. 5: C-Group, Pan-Grave and Kerma Remains at Adindan Cemeteries T, K, U, and J*. Chicago, 1989.

Woolley, C.L. *Karanog – The Town*. Eckley B. Coxe Junior Expedition to Nubia V. Philadelphia, 1911.

Woolley, C.L. and D. Randall-Maciver. *Karanog – The Romano-Nubian Cemetery*. 2

volumes, Text and Plates. Eckley B. Coxe Junior Expedition to Nubia III. Philadelphia, 1911.

Yousif el Amin. *Later Pleistocene Cultural Adaptations in Sudanese Nubia*. Cambridge
Monographs in African Archaeology 4. BAR International Series 114. Oxford
1981.

Yousif el Amin. 'The Late Paleolithic in Sudan in the Light of new data from the
Atbara.' *Nubian Culture Past and Present*, ed. T. Hägg. Stockholm, 1987, 33–46.

INDEX

A-Group 39, 43–4, Map 4, 46, 47, 50–3, 54, 55–6, 59, 63, 64, 70, 71
Abdullab 133–4
Abkan 40, 48
Abri 8
Abu 64, 65
Abu Fatma 13
Abu Hamed 7
Aburni 122
Abu Simbel 83, 92
Abydos 72
Acheulean 17, Fig.4, 21, 26
Adams, W.Y. 44, 53
Adendan 130
Afia 46
Agordat 55
Ahmose, pharaoh 80
Ahmose son of Ebana 79, 80, 81
Akhenaten 86, 87, 91
Akhmim 125
Aksha 92
Alara 97
al-Baladhuri 123
Alexander the Great 103
Alodia 122
al-'Omari 129
Alwa 122, 133
Amada 58, Fig.16, 63, 83, 89
Amani-nete-yerike 102, 105
Amanishkhete 114, 116
Amanislo 108
Amanitare 110, 111, 112, 113, 116
Amara 113
Amara West 82, 85
Amennemes I 72

Amennemes III 70, 73
Amenophis I 80, 86
Amenophis II 83, 89, 96
Amenophis III 83, 86
Amr ibn al-'As 123
Amun, god 87, 92, 93, 99, 100, 101, 102, 105, 108, 111, 114
Aniba 12, 56, 72, 77, 82, 83, 89, 100
angareeb 100
Anlamani 101
Apedemek, god 111, 112, 114
Archaeological Survey of Nubia 43
Arakakamani 105, 108
Arensnuphis 113
Arikhankharer 111, 114
Argo island 87, 113
Arkell, A.J. 26, 27, 28, 30, 34, 35, 36
Arnekhamani 111
Arqamani 106, 112
Askut 73
Aspelta 102, 106
Assyria 100
Aswan 1, 3, 6, 9, 12, 13, 43, 46, 50, 64, 65, 91, 92, 93, 106, 116, 119, 132
Asyut 70
Atbara 14, 117, 122
Atbara, river 6, 81
Aten 86
Atlanersa 101, 106
Augustus 116, 120
Auserra, king (Auserre) 79
Axum 116, 117
Ayyubid 132

Baghdad 129

141

B-Group 43, 52
Ballana 118, 122
Ballanan 25
Banu Kanz 133
baqt 124
barley 62
Bartare 108
Batn el Hagar 8
Bayuda 8, 102
Bauga 7
Begarawiya 105
Beit el Wali 93
Bega 67, 118, 122, 125
Beybars 133
Bietak, M. 54
Birgid language 12
Blemmyes 118, 119
Blue Nile 1, 5, 27, 55, 117, 122
Boston 100
Buhen 63, 64, 72, 73, 83, 99
Butana 7, 10, 33
Byzantine 120
Byzantium 122

C-Group 43, 52, 54, 55, 57, 58, 59, 62, 65, 67,
   70, 72, 77, 78, 82, 89, 90, 95, 98, 102, 103, 114
camel 11
Caneva, I. 30
Capsian 25
Cataracts: First 1, 64; Second 8, 9, 73; Third 1,
   103; Fourth 1; Sixth 6; Dal 8
Chalcedon, Council of 120
Chephren (Khaefra) 63
Clark, J.D. 32
Climate 11
Coptic church 120, 121
Coptic inscriptions 122

Dabenarti 73
Daju language 12
Dakka 112
Danagla 3
Darfur 12
David, king 133
Debba 1, 13, 26
Debeira East 57, 89, 126
Debeira West 125–6, 131
Deffufa, East 67, 68
Deffufa, West 67, 68, 81
Deir-el-Medina 86, 100
Delgo 8
Dendur 120, 123
Derr 93, 94
Dinder, river 5

Dinka 33
Diocletian 118, 126
Diodorus Siculus 106, 116
Djehuty-hetep 89
Djer, king 51, Fig.12, 43
Dodecaschoinus 112
Dongola 8, 33, 87, 98, 113, 124–5, 130, 132–3
Dongalawi language 13
Do-tawo 133
Dynasties: Sixth 91; Eleventh 72; Twelfth 85;
   Thirteenth 77; Eighteenth 58, 72, 86;
   Nineteenth 91; Twentieth 86; Twenty-
   second 94

'Early Khartoum' 28, 33, 35
Eastern Sudanic languages 12
Edfu 125
Eirpanome 120, 126
Elephantine 64, 65, 98
El Hakim el Mansur 131
El Kab 79
'El Malik Group' 42
Emery, W.B. 64, 83
Eparch 130
Ergamenes 106
Eritrea 55
Ermenna 125
Esarhaddon 100
Ethiopia 5, 65, 116
Ezana 116, 117

Fadija language 13
Faras 112–13, 120, 122–5, 128, 130–1
Fatimids 129
Fekri Hassan 21
Firka 118
First Intermediate 54, 91
Fostat 125
Fung 134

Garba 112
Gash, river 72
Gebel Adda 126, 131, 133
Gebel Auliya 6
Gebel Barkal 7, 87, 89, 94, 95, 97–9, 100–3, 105,
   113
Gebel Qeili 10, 112
Gebel Moya 112
Gebel Rowyan 6
Gebel Sahaba 25
Gebel Sheikh Suleiman 51
Geili 36, 37
Gemai 118
Gemaian 24

Gem Aten 87
George, son of Zakaria 129
Gerf Hussein 93
Gezira 5, 9, 11
Ghazali 131
Giza 63
'gouges' 35
Gratien, B. 72
Greek inscriptions 118, 122

Haaland, R. 37
hafir 112
Halfa Degheim 49
Halfan 25
Hambukol 10
Harkhuf 64, 65, 68
Harsiotef 102, 113
Hathor, goddess 93
Hatshepsut 85
Hattusilis II 92
Heka-nefer 89, 91
Hepjefa 70
Herihor 94
Hermopolis (Eshmunein) 99
Herodotus 116
High Dam 3, 13
Hobagi 117
Horemheb 87, 91, 92
Horus, god 85, 91
Hu 67
Humay 91
Huy 90
Hyksos 70, 77, 78, 79

Ibrahim el Kurdi 130
Iken 76
Ikhmindi 126, 131
Ikkur 72, 77, 83
Irem 91
Iri 64
Irtjet 66
Isis, goddess 114
Islam 119
Islang 38

Jaaliyyin 14
John the Deacon 124
Julian 122
Justinian 120, 122

Kadero 36, 37, 38
Kadesh 92
Kalabsha 7, 9, 118
Kamose 79

Kandake 116
Karanog 112
'Karat Group' 42
Karnak 81, 99
Karima 8
Kashta 97, 98, 99
Kawa 87, 101, 102, 103, 105, 113
Kedada 39
Kemp, B. 85
Kendall, T. 100
Kenuz 3, 13, 132
Kenuz language 12
Keraba 7, 9, 111, 112
Kerma 13, 62, 67, Fig.18, 70, 71, 72, 77, 78, 81,
    82, 86, 87, 90, 97, 98, 102, 103
Khaefra (Chephren) 63
Khandaq 129
Khartoum 1, 3, 5, 10, 12, 14, 17, 27, 30, 85
Khartoum hospital 28, 30, 32, 36
Khartoum Mesolithic 28
Khartoum 'variant' 34, 40
Khor Abu Anga 17
Khor Nubt 126
Khormusan 24
Kom Ombo 1, 13, 125
Kor 73
Kordofan 12
Korti 8
Kubania 44
Kubban 83
Kudanbes, king 133
Kumma 73, 85
Kurgus 81, fig.21, 87
Kurru 97, 98, 101, 102, 105
Kush 3, 70, 78, 79, 81, 82, 85, 91, 94, 114

Lake Nasser 1
Lake Nubia 1
Lake Tana 5
Latin inscription 111
Levallois 24
Libyans 94
Longinus 122
Luxor 86

Mahas 3, 13, 126
Mainarti 125–6, 131
Makuria 122, 124, 128
Mamluks 130, 132
Medjay 67, 73, 91, 118
Meidobi language 12
Mekher 65
Melkite church 122
Memphis 65, 67, 99

Men-Ra-sehetep-en-Amun 94
Merkurios 124, 128
Mernera 64
Meroe 8, 14, 102, 103, 105, 106, 107, Map 8, 110, 112, 113, 114, 116, 117, 118
Meroitic writing 114
Merowe 8
Miam (Aniba) 89
Middle Kingdom 54, 68, 70, 72, 78, 83, 84, 85
millet 10
Mirgissa 73, 76
Missimina 103
Mousterian 21, Fig.6, 24
Musawwarat es Sofra fig.28, 111, 113
Muttuy 92

Nahum, prophet 100
'Naima' pottery 32
Namlot 99
Napata 95, 96, 97, 99, 100, 102, 103, 117
Naqa 111, 112, 113, 114
Naqada 44
Nastasen 100, 102
nbw 3
Nefertari 92, 93
nehesi 76, 94
Netekamani 109, 111, 112, 113, 116
New Kingdom 54, 78, 81, 82, 86, 87, 89, 100, 113
Nilo-Saharan languages 12
Nobiin 3
Nofalab 38
Noba 117, 118, 119
Nobatae 117, 118, 119, 120, 122
Nobatia 118, 122, 124, 128, 130
Nuba 1
Nubian language 1, 3, 12, 118, 120, 133
Nubian mercenaries 61
Nubian physical types 13
Nuri 101, 102, 105, 113, 114

O'Connor, D. 65
Old Dongola 119, 122–4, 129, 133
Old Kingdom 52, 53, 54, 55, 64, 68, 72, 82, 91
Old Nubian 111, 126
Old Nubian writing 126–7
Omdurman Bridge 39, 55
Osiris, god 92

Palestine 82
Pan-graves 66, Map 5, 67, 91
Paulos, bishop 125, 128
Penehesi 94
Pennut 94

Pepi I 68
Pepi II 65, 66, 68
Pepi-Nakht 65
Petrie, Flinders 67
Philae 106, 112, 120
Piankhy (Piye) 98, 99, 100, 101, 105
Pliny 116
Procopius 118
Psammetichus II 92, 102, 106
Ptah, god 93
Ptolemy II 106
Ptolemy IV 106
Publius Petronius 116
Punt 65

Qadan 25, 40
Qasr Ibrim 10, 11, 99, 112, 118, 126, 130–1
Qere 116
Qerri 133
Quban 72
Qustul 50, 51, 117

Rahad, river 5
Ramesses II 83, 85, 87, 92, 93, 126
Ramesses III 93, 94
Ramesses VI 94
Raphael, king 129
Red Sea 67
Red Sea Hills 125
Re-Harakhte, god 92, 93
Reisner, G.A. 43, 52, 70, 97, 106, 117
Rekhmire 89
rhyolite 36

Sabaloka 6
Sadenga 85, 86, 101, 113
Saggai 28, 30, 32
Sai 72, 85, 86, 91
Salah-el-Din 130
Samos 116
Sanam 102, 103
saqia 8, 10
Saras 46
Sarurab 28, 32
Sayala 46, 50, 52, 56, 57
Sebilian 24, 25
Sebiumeker, god 113
Sebni 65, 70
Second Intermediate 54, 57, 70, 72
seluka 10
Semna 8, 73, 76, 80, 85, 94, 99
Seneca 116
Senkamanisken 101, 105
Sennar 1, 3, 5, 134

Sennuwy 69
Sesebi 85, 86, Fig.23
Sesostris I 70, 72, 73
Sesostris III 73, 76, 85, 91
Setaw 93
Seti I 91, 92, 93
Shabako 99
Shabona 28, 32
Shebitku 99
Shaheinab 34, 35, 36, 38, 39
Shaiqiya 14
Shaqadud 28, 33, 38, 39, 40
Sheikh Daud 47
Shekanda 133
Shelfak 73
Shendi 6, 26
Sherkarer 112
Shilluk 33
Shoshenq I 94
Sikkat el Maheila 87
Silko 118, 119, 122
Silsila 91
Sinkat 126
Soba 119, 122, 125, 133–4
Soleb 85, 86
Solomon, king 129
sorghum 5, 9, 10
Strabo 116
Synodontis schall (catfish) 28
Syria 82, 92

Tabo 87, 113
Tagra 28, 32
Taharqa 99, 100, 101, 102, 113
Taifa 124
Talmis 118
Tanqasi 117
Tanwetamani 100, 101
Tanyidamani 114
Taphis 118
Ta-sety 3
Tefnakhte 99
Teqerideamani 106
'Tergis group' 42

Thebes 78, 99, 100
Theodore, Bishop 122
Thryonomis swinderianus (cane rat) 28
Thuwra 80, 82
Tiye, queen 86
Tokiltoeton 126
Toshka 63
Trigger, B.G. 56
Tshitolian 24
Tumbus 81
Turan Shah 130
Turkish times 86
Tutankhamen 83, 87, 89, 90
Tuthmosis I 80, 81, 83
Tuthmosis II 81
Tuthmosis III 81, 83, 85, 87, 89
Tuthmosis IV 82, 87

Umara Dunqas 134
Umm Direiwa 37, 38
'Uqba ibn Nafi' 123
Uronarti 73, 80, 85
Ushara 38

Vercoutter, J. 86

Wad ben Naqa 112
Wadi Abu Dom 8
Wadi Allaqi 83
Wadi Halfa 7, 8, 11, 12, 17, 24, 33, 51, 126
Wadi el Sebua 57, Fig.13, 58, 83, 93, 112, 126
'Wavy line' culture 28
Wawat 66, 72, 82, 91, 94
Wendorf, F. 21
White Nile 1, 5, 27, 28, 55, 117
Williams, B. 50
Wizz 131

X-Group 43, 117, 122

Yam 64, 65, 68, 70
Yousef el Amin 12

Zakaria, king 129
Zakiab 37